Vanished – The Shocking Murder of Gabby Petito

An American True Crime Tragedy

Jack Hunter

© Copyright 2025 - All rights reserved.

The content contained within this book may not be reproduced, duplicated or transmitted without direct written permission from the author or the publisher.

Under no circumstances will any blame or legal responsibility be held against the publisher, or author, for any damages, reparation, or monetary loss due to the information contained within this book, either directly or indirectly.

Legal Notice:

This book is copyright protected. It is only for personal use. You cannot amend, distribute, sell, use, quote or paraphrase any part, or the content within this book, without the consent of the author or publisher.

Disclaimer Notice:

Please note the information contained within this document is for educational and entertainment purposes only. All effort has been executed to present accurate, up to date, reliable, complete information. No warranties of any kind are declared or implied. Readers acknowledge that the author is not engaging in the rendering of legal, financial, medical or professional advice. The content within this book has been derived from various sources. Please consult a licensed professional before attempting any techniques outlined in this book.

By reading this document, the reader agrees that under no circumstances is the author responsible for any losses, direct or indirect, that are incurred as a result of the use of information contained within this document, including, but not limited to, errors, omissions, or inaccuracies.

Contents

Introduction		1
1.	Gabby and Brian A Social Media Persona	2
2.	The CrossCountry Road Trip Early Warning Signs	5
3.	Escalating Tensions Moab Incident	8
4.	The Last Communication A Digital Breadcrumb Trail	11
5.	The Disappearance A Nations Attention	14
6.	The Search for Gabby A MultiAgency Effort	17
7.	Brian Laundrie The Suspect Emerges	20
8.	Forensic Evidence The Physical Clues	23
9.	Digital Forensics The Online Trail	26
10.	The Discovery of Gabby's Remains A Grim Confirmation	29
11.	The Power of Social Media A Double Edged Sword	32
12.	The News Cycle Sensationalism vs Responsibility	35
13.	The Role of Online Communities Support and Speculation	38
14.	Public Outrage and the Demand for Justice	41
15.	The Aftermath Lessons Learned and Future Implications	44
16.	Understanding the Dynamics of Abuse A Cycle of Violence	47
17.	Identifying Red Flags Verbal Emotional and Physical Abuse	50
18.	The Impact of Isolation and Control Tactics of Abuse	53
19.	Breaking the Cycle Support Systems and Resources	56
20.	Prevention and Intervention A Community Responsibility	59
21.	Remembering Gabby Beyond the Headlines	62
22.	The Impact on Domestic Violence Awareness	65

23.	Reforming Law Enforcement Response to Domestic Violence	68
24.	Improving Support for Victims of Domestic Violence	71
25.	The Enduring Legacy of Gabby A Call to Action	74

Introduction

The summer of 2021 saw the story of Gabby Petito explode across social media and news outlets, transforming a missing person's case into a national phenomenon. Her cross-country van life adventure with her fiancé, Brian Laundrie, quickly transitioned from an idyllic depiction of freedom and exploration to a harrowing mystery that gripped the nation. The meticulously crafted online persona the couple projected starkly contrasted with the chilling reality of their deteriorating relationship, a reality hinted at through subtle cracks in their digital footprint. This book aims to unravel the layers of this tragic story, providing a comprehensive account grounded in meticulous research and a deep dive into the available evidence. We will trace Gabby and Brian's journey, analyzing the seemingly insignificant moments, the escalating tensions, and the critical missed opportunities that ultimately led to Gabby's untimely death. Beyond the sensationalized headlines, this book aims to understand the warning signs that might have been recognized, the role of social media in shaping public perception and fueling the investigation, and the complexities of the law enforcement response. It explores the digital breadcrumb trail left behind – the social media posts, text messages, and GPS data – piecing together the events of her final days. This investigation goes beyond the surface, examining the dynamics of domestic violence, the power of online communities, and the profound impact of this case on the national conversation about justice and accountability. The goal is to not only understand what happened to Gabby Petito, but to use her story as a catalyst for change, highlighting the need for improved domestic violence awareness, prevention, and response.

Chapter One

Gabby and Brian A Social Media Persona

The meticulously curated Instagram feed, a vibrant tapestry woven with sun-drenched landscapes and beaming smiles, initially presented a picture-perfect portrayal of Gabby and Brian's van life adventure. Each post, a carefully composed vignette, showcased their idyllic journey across the American West: breathtaking vistas of national parks, cozy nights spent nestled in their converted van, and adventurous hikes through rugged terrain. Gabby, with her infectious laugh and adventurous spirit, emerged as the radiant star, her presence radiating positivity and wanderlust. Brian, often captured in the background, played the supportive role, the silent partner in this meticulously crafted narrative of freedom and exploration. Their joint account, brimming with professionally edited photos and engaging captions, painted a picture of a couple deeply in love, embarking on a once-in- a-lifetime adventure.

A closer examination, however, reveals subtle cracks in this seemingly flawless facade. While the surface level depicted a harmonious union, a deeper dive into their digital footprint unveils a more complex reality. The frequency of their posts, initially consistent and regular, began to dwindle as their journey progressed. The carefree smiles, once abundant, became less frequent, replaced by a more strained and forced demeanor captured in certain photographs. Body language, a silent language often overlooked in digital analysis, speaks volumes. In several images, Gabby's posture appears tense, her eyes lacking the usual sparkle. These subtle shifts, barely perceptible at first glance, hint at an underlying tension, a discordance between the idealized image projected online and the reality of their relationship.

The captions accompanying their posts, initially filled with exuberance and excitement, also undergo a gradual transformation. Early entries overflowed with shared joy and anticipation, detailing planned activities and expressing gratitude for their shared experience. As time progresses, however, the tone shifts subtly. The captions become shorter, less descriptive, and less emotionally charged. The vibrant, playful banter that once characterized their interactions gives way to more generic statements, lacking the spontaneity and intimacy that defined their early posts. This gradual erosion of emotional expression, a silent narrative unfolding across their social media presence, provides a chilling counterpoint to the carefully constructed illusion of marital bliss.

Detailed analysis of the individual photographs offers further insights. While the overall aesthetic maintained a consistent level of professionalism, inconsistencies begin to emerge upon closer scrutiny. In some images, Gabby's face bears traces of exhaustion or distress, a stark contrast to the vibrant smiles displayed in others. The meticulous editing, previously consistent, reveals subtle inconsistencies in lighting and color grading, hinting at hasty post-production efforts or perhaps, a desperate attempt to mask something hidden beneath the carefully curated surface. Certain photos, initially included in the feed and then later deleted, further fuel suspicion. While the reasons for their removal remain unclear, it is impossible to ignore the implication of a deliberate attempt to scrub their digital history, raising questions about the true nature of their relationship.

The use of specific hashtags also offers a revealing glimpse into the couple's evolving emotional state. Early posts were brimming with positive hashtags reflecting their adventurous lifestyle: #vanlife, #exploremore, #couplegoals, #travelgram. As their journey progresses, however, these upbeat hashtags become less prevalent, replaced by more somber and introspective ones – tags that subtly hint at underlying anxieties: #findingmyself, #selfdiscovery, #innerpeace, #seekingbalance. The shift in hashtag selection suggests a growing internal conflict, a growing dissatisfaction with their current reality, starkly contrasted with the idyllic image presented in the accompanying photographs.

Beyond the visual cues and carefully crafted captions, the comments section of their posts also offers a fertile ground for investigation. While most comments expressed admiration for their adventurous lifestyle and expressed envy for their journey, a few stood out as subtly unsettling. Several comments, now deleted, pointed out inconsistencies in Gabby's demeanor, expressing concern about her seeming distress or unhappiness. These comments, initially dismissed as mere speculation, gain a new significance in hindsight, serving as unwitting indicators of an underlying discord that would ultimately lead to tragedy. The fact that they were later deleted further suggests a calculated attempt to control their online narrative, to suppress any hint of discord or discontent within their supposedly perfect relationship.

Analyzing the metadata embedded within the images and videos further adds to the narrative. GPS coordinates embedded in some posts reveal unexpected deviations from their purported itinerary, suggesting unplanned stops or detours that remain unexplained. The timestamps attached to various posts and stories reveal inconsistencies in the timeline of their journey, raising questions about the accuracy of their meticulously crafted online narrative. This discrepancy between the idealized online journey and the reality of their travels serves as another critical piece of the puzzle, suggesting a deliberate attempt to mislead their online audience about their actual location and activities.

Furthermore, an examination of Brian's individual social media activity reveals a different narrative, one that contrasts sharply with the shared accounts they maintained. While his public posts maintained the facade of a supportive partner, his private messages, if recovered through legal channels, might offer a very different perspective. The absence of updates during critical periods, combined with an apparent lack of engagement in responding to comments on Gabby's posts, hints at a detachment and lack of emotional involvement that runs counter to the idyllic image they collectively presented to the world. The contrast between their public image and private behaviors underscores the importance of examining digital footprints for inconsistencies and subtle cues of hidden realities.

The interaction patterns between Gabby and Brian on social media also warrant a thorough examination. While the shared account promoted a harmonious partnership, a closer examination of their individual posts, likes, and comments suggests a less idyllic reality. The lack of interaction, or the presence of strained interactions, particularly in the weeks leading up to Gabby's disappearance, could signify a breakdown in communication or a potential escalation of conflict. This could be further analyzed by comparing the dates and times of their posts with other evidence such as credit card transactions or GPS data to establish a more detailed timeline.

The seemingly innocuous details – the sudden shift in photo aesthetics, the subtle changes in captions, the inconsistent posting frequency, the deleted comments – all add up to a disquieting picture. These subtle cues, often overlooked in a casual perusal of social media, reveal a far more complex and troubling reality beneath the surface of their carefully crafted online persona. The meticulously constructed image of a happy couple embarking on an adventurous journey masks a far more sinister and tragic reality, a reality that only begins to come into focus when one delves beyond the superficial charm of their social media presence. The digital footprint, initially appearing to be a testament to a perfect relationship, ultimately serves as a crucial piece of evidence, providing chilling hints of the impending tragedy that would befall Gabby Petito. The seemingly idyllic van life dream, meticulously documented on social media, would soon transform into a nightmare, a story that would unfold not only on the dusty roads of America but also on the digital landscapes of the internet.

Chapter Two

The CrossCountry Road Trip Early Warning Signs

The meticulously planned itinerary, a testament to Gabby's organizational skills, initially unfolded without significant incident. Their journey began in New York, a departure marked by an enthusiastic flurry of Instagram posts showcasing their newly converted van, christened "The Wanderer." The early days were a blur of excitement, captured in vibrant photos and videos that chronicled their progress across the eastern states. Each stop, from bustling cityscapes to quaint roadside diners, was documented with meticulous detail, creating a near-perfect digital diary of their adventure. The early posts revealed a couple seemingly deeply in love, their interactions playful and affectionate, their shared enthusiasm palpable through the screen.

However, subtle discordant notes began to appear, barely perceptible at first, but growing more pronounced as their journey progressed. While the Instagram feed maintained its outwardly positive façade, a closer analysis reveals a gradual shift in the couple's dynamic. The initial exuberance gave way to a more subdued energy, noticeable in the decreased frequency of posts and the shift in the tone of captions. The playful banter that had characterized their early interactions was replaced by a more formal, almost stilted communication style.

Their first significant stop, in the Shenandoah National Park in Virginia, marked a turning point. While the photos presented a picturesque image of a couple enjoying nature, a video captured a brief argument, albeit a seemingly trivial one, concerning the route and their next destination. The video, initially posted as a "funny" moment on Brian's private Instagram story, was later deleted – a detail that, in hindsight, becomes increasingly significant. This seemingly minor disagreement, however, served as a precursor to more serious incidents that would punctuate their journey across the country.

The next leg of their journey took them through the Great Smoky Mountains National Park in North Carolina and Tennessee. Here, reports from fellow campers and park rangers suggest a growing tension between the couple. Several witnesses reported witnessing elevated voices and heated exchanges, although none witnessed any physical violence. These accounts, documented in police reports later obtained, paint a picture of a relationship increasingly frayed at the edges.

Their westward journey continued, taking them through several states, each stop marked by a similar pattern. The meticulously curated Instagram posts continued, presenting a picture-perfect image, yet the underlying reality, pieced together from police reports, witness statements, and a painstaking analysis of their digital footprint, painted a far more disturbing picture. In Utah, several encounters with local law enforcement became more significant than the initial press accounts revealed. A minor traffic stop, initially dismissed as a routine event, reveals through police dashcam footage, subtle signs of tension and discord between the couple. Gabby's body language, visible even through the low-resolution footage, suggests a discomfort and unease that contradicts the image presented in their later social media posts. Similarly, police recordings from the interaction reveal a brief, hushed argument concerning their itinerary. These seemingly inconsequential events accumulate, building a narrative of increasing stress and conflict.

Their time in Arches and Canyonlands National Parks in Utah is particularly revealing. Here, the photographs portray a breathtaking backdrop but fail to capture the internal struggles playing out between the couple. While the majestic landscapes provided a visually stunning backdrop for their social media posts, evidence suggests that their relationship was undergoing a significant deterioration. Witnesses recall seeing Gabby visibly upset, isolated from Brian, expressing frustration and anger. At this point, the carefully crafted façade was starting to crumble.

As they moved further west into Colorado, the pattern continued, with more frequent arguments documented by witnesses and documented via cell phone records and location data which correlated with their erratic route changes. Texts retrieved from Gabby's phone, after a legal battle to access her data, show a growing sense of unease and frustration in her messages to friends and family. She expresses concern about Brian's behavior, although her communications lack explicit details, a detail which speaks to potential safety concerns inhibiting her from being completely open and honest in her communications. A series of increasingly cryptic messages suggest a rising level of distress, even though none describe any explicit threat of violence.

The journey through the stunning landscapes of Wyoming was marked by a near-total silence on social media. The regular updates ceased abruptly. The perfectly planned itinerary disintegrated. While some suggest this might just be a technical hiccup in a remote area with poor cell service, in hindsight, this lack of updates, along with the lack of phone communication, signals a significant break in their previously documented consistent activity and communication. The absence of posts, however, provided only a glimpse into the escalating crisis.

An examination of their credit card transactions and GPS data further contributes to building the timeline of the journey and provides insight into their whereabouts, especially in the days leading up to Gabby's disappearance. The inconsistencies between their self-reported locations and the data extracted from their banking records and phone metadata raise serious concerns. These discrepancies, however, only highlight the growing gaps in the narrative that needed to be further investigated.

The final leg of their journey, in Grand Teton National Park, proved to be the most critical. While the couple's interactions remained largely undocumented in social media, interviews conducted with local businesses and nearby campers revealed increasing signs of conflict. This included a noticeable absence of Gabby, with Brian often seen alone, his demeanor described as anxious and evasive. A review of the security footage from various establishments, including gas stations and cafes they frequented, reveal more evidence of the couple's tense and argumentative interactions. The videos, though of low quality, clearly show signs of unease and potential aggressive behaviors.

This meticulous piecing together of fragments—from social media posts to police reports, witness accounts to credit card transactions—builds a comprehensive narrative of a cross- country journey that began as an idyllic dream but descended into a tragic nightmare. The early warning signs, subtle at first, accumulate into a damning indictment of a relationship marked by increasing conflict and a chilling foreshadowing of the devastating events to come. The meticulously crafted Instagram feed, initially a seemingly perfect portrayal of a carefree couple, now stands as a chilling record of the deterioration of a relationship and a foreboding portrait of the tragedy that would soon unfold. The idyllic van life dream was shattered, leaving a trail of digital breadcrumbs leading investigators and the public towards the grim truth.

Chapter Three

Escalating Tensions Moab Incident

The seemingly idyllic journey took a significant turn in Moab, Utah. On August 12th, 2021, a 911 call reporting a domestic disturbance involving a young couple in a white Ford Transit van would irrevocably alter the course of Gabby and Brian's trip, and indeed, their lives. The call, originating from a witness who observed a young man slapping a young woman, initiated a chain of events that, while not immediately resulting in arrests or serious consequences, would later become a focal point in the investigation into Gabby's disappearance.

The responding Moab City Police officers arrived on the scene and encountered Gabby and Brian. The body camera footage, released to the public following a protracted legal battle, offers a chilling glimpse into the interaction. The video, grainy and at times difficult to decipher due to the low-light conditions and distance, captures fragmented exchanges between the officers, Gabby, and Brian. Gabby, visibly upset and tearful, recounts an altercation. She describes a struggle over her phone, explaining that Brian had attempted to prevent her from contacting her family. Her account, punctuated by sobs and emotionally charged statements, details a pattern of conflict during their journey. She described feeling overwhelmed and stressed, citing specific instances of Brian's behavior causing her anxiety and frustration.

The body cam footage meticulously records the officers' attempts to establish the facts of the situation. They question both Gabby and Brian separately, attempting to elicit details about the alleged altercation and gauge the level of danger present. Brian offers a seemingly coherent account of the incident, framing the conflict as a disagreement that escalated but did not involve physical violence. His demeanor in the video is a stark contrast to Gabby's emotional distress, remaining calm and collected throughout the interaction.

The contrast between Gabby and Brian's accounts creates a significant narrative tension. Gabby's emotional distress is palpable, her words suggesting a history of controlling behavior on Brian's part. Her statement speaks of feeling manipulated and intimidated, yet her description of the physical altercation lacked the clarity or detail that would explicitly indicate a severe assault. Brian, in contrast, is calm and collected, almost too calm, prompting questions about the veracity of his account and possibly indicating an attempt at downplaying or minimizing the severity of the situation.

Crucially, the dispatch notes from the 911 call and the subsequent police reports are equally revealing. The dispatcher's initial account outlines the details of the call – a witness reporting witnessing a man slapping a woman, the potential for a domestic dispute, and the description of the vehicle involved. This independent corroboration of Gabby's account adds a layer of credibility to her claims, even if it remains short of definitive proof of physical violence. Furthermore, the police reports themselves, including the officers' detailed observations and assessment of the situation, provide a critical record of the event and their subsequent handling of it.

The police officers involved spent significant time assessing the situation. They attempted to determine whether any physical violence had occurred and gauge the overall level of risk to Gabby. The evaluation process, as seen through the body cam footage, is not quick or straightforward. The officers visibly wrestled with their assessment, weighing Gabby's emotional distress against Brian's relatively calm demeanor. Their decision not to make an arrest was a critical turning point, and one that would later become a point of significant scrutiny.

Following the incident, the officers separated Gabby and Brian, giving them space to de-escalate. They offered both parties resources and advice. While they did not pursue criminal charges, they clearly documented the event and their subsequent interactions with both individuals, including their observations and assessments. This documentation, while providing a record of the event, would later be critically analyzed for any possible failures in assessing the situation and applying appropriate protocols for handling domestic violence calls.

Expert opinions on police procedure and domestic violence response are crucial to understanding the implications of the Moab incident. Many experts in law enforcement and domestic violence intervention, when reviewing the footage and police reports, have raised concerns about the officers' handling of the situation. The decision not to press charges, given Gabby's visible distress and account of Brian's controlling behavior, has been viewed by some as a missed opportunity to intervene and prevent further escalation.

The lack of clear evidence of physical assault, while seemingly justifying the decision not to arrest Brian, ignores the broader context of emotional abuse and coercive control. Many domestic violence incidents do not involve obvious physical injuries, yet the underlying dynamics of power and control can be equally harmful. Experts suggest that police officers need more comprehensive training to identify and effectively respond to such instances, recognizing the signs of emotional abuse and coercive control beyond the visible evidence of physical violence.

The Moab incident highlights the complexities involved in responding to domestic violence calls. It presents a nuanced situation where the subjective interpretation of the events and the lack of easily identifiable physical injuries led to a decision that, in hindsight, has drawn significant criticism. The lack of arrest, the separation, and the advice offered – all became subjects of scrutiny.

Whether the officers' handling of the situation constitutes negligence or a simple misjudgment of a complex situation is a matter of debate and subject to differing interpretations. However, it is clear that the events in Moab played a crucial role in the overall narrative, highlighting the potential consequences of misinterpretations in domestic violence calls and underscoring the importance of comprehensive training and protocols for police officers. The seemingly minor incident in Moab would ultimately have lasting and tragic consequences. The lack of intervention, the decision not to arrest, the perceived dismissal of Gabby's concerns - all of these would contribute to the tragic narrative that would unfold in the weeks to come. The seemingly minor incident in Moab would ultimately have lasting and tragic consequences. The lack of intervention, the decision not to arrest, the perceived dismissal of Gabby's concerns - all of these would contribute to the tragic narrative that would unfold in the weeks to come. The Moab incident serves as a poignant reminder of the complexities of domestic violence and the critical need for improved training and interventions. Its implications extend beyond the immediate event, sparking broader conversations about police procedures, domestic violence awareness, and the critical importance of recognizing and responding to signs of abuse, regardless of the presence of readily apparent physical injury. The case underscores the tragic consequences of missed opportunities for intervention and the need for more effective strategies to protect victims of domestic abuse.

Chapter Four

The Last Communication A Digital Breadcrumb Trail

The investigation into Gabby Petito's disappearance relied heavily on the digital breadcrumbs she and Brian Laundrie left behind. Their constant sharing on social media, a hallmark of their van life adventure, ironically became a crucial tool in piecing together the final days of her life. While the vibrant, seemingly carefree images and videos projected an image of idyllic travel, a closer examination reveals a subtle shift in tone, a creeping unease detectable only through careful scrutiny of the metadata and subtle cues embedded within the digital record.

Gabby's last known communication with her mother, Nichole Schmidt, occurred on August 27th, 2021. This text message, short and seemingly innocuous, read simply, "Can you help Stan, I'll call you tonight." The reference to "Stan" is believed to be a nickname for her grandfather, suggesting a possible family errand or matter requiring her mother's assistance. The message itself appears normal, devoid of any overt hints of distress. However, the timing is significant.

This was the last direct communication Gabby had with her mother, a jarring silence that immediately raised red flags when she failed to appear at scheduled video calls. Further analysis of the message's metadata—the timestamps and location data associated with the message—could help investigators determine the precise location from which it was sent, potentially corroborating other evidence regarding Gabby and Brian's movements. Furthermore, the apparent urgency suggested by her request for immediate assistance and the unfulfilled promise of a later phone call creates a subtle sense of foreboding.

A deeper dive into Gabby's social media activity reveals a similar pattern. Her Instagram posts, usually frequent and filled with vibrant photos of stunning landscapes and their travels, became noticeably less frequent in the days leading up to her disappearance. The final posts, while seemingly cheerful, lacked the usual exuberance and spontaneity. A closer look at the geotagging data associated with these posts, and a cross-reference with the metadata of her text messages and phone records, can help investigators piece together the precise route Gabby and Brian took. Any discrepancies or inconsistencies between her online activity and the official timeline of their journey could reveal potential areas of interest that warrant further investigation. The images themselves, seemingly trivial at first glance, could harbor subtle clues, a change in facial expression, a subtle shift in body language, a strained smile hinting at underlying tension. Experienced digital forensic analysts scrutinized each image, searching for details the naked eye might miss – a reflection in sunglasses, a shadow cast in a certain way, or an object in the background that might offer an additional context.

Brian Laundrie's own digital footprint became a critical piece of the puzzle. His silence in the days after Gabby's disappearance was particularly unsettling. While he initially declined to cooperate with law enforcement and returned to his family home in Florida alone, driving Gabby's van, his digital silence was a stark contrast to the constant flow of online activity from the couple's shared account during their travels. A meticulous analysis of his social media activity, including any comments, posts, or engagement with online news surrounding the disappearance, could shed light on his state of mind and his possible involvement in Gabby's disappearance. Any attempts to delete or modify social media activity also came under scrutiny. Law enforcement agencies work closely with digital forensic experts to analyze data for any sign of tampering, deletion, or manipulation that could indicate concealment of evidence. The timeline of his digital activity, viewed in conjunction with the timeline of Gabby's communication, offered insights into the possibility of discrepancies and inconsistencies that warrant further investigation.

The GPS data from their rental van proved invaluable. This data, obtained through a subpoena from the rental company, detailed their precise route throughout their trip. By analyzing the GPS coordinates and comparing them to the timeline of Gabby's last communications, investigators could establish the exact locations where they were at key moments. A significant portion of this data was obscured or unavailable, which immediately raised the suspicion that data had been intentionally deleted, corrupted, or manipulated. These gaps in the digital trail often are more significant than the available data itself, offering hints of potentially deliberate actions undertaken to obfuscate the chronology of events. The reconstruction of their movements based on available GPS data became critical for determining the precise location of the last known communication and mapping the likely trajectory of their journey in the days leading up to Gabby's disappearance.

The cellphone records of both Gabby and Brian, including call logs, text messages, and location data from their mobile devices, provided a detailed narrative of their interactions. Law enforcement agencies often utilize a technique known as cell site analysis, which uses cellular tower data to triangulate the location of a phone at a given time. This analysis, when combined with the GPS data from the van, can create a comprehensive map of their movements, filling in potential gaps left by incomplete or manipulated GPS data. The content of their calls and texts, analyzed with the use of sophisticated linguistics tools, could reveal subtle shifts in tone, frequency, or content that might indicate escalating tensions or conflicts in their relationship. The frequency and timing of calls between Gabby and her family, compared to those between Brian and his family, could offer key insights into the dynamics of their relationship and the degree of isolation Gabby may have experienced in the final days.

The digital evidence, when meticulously pieced together, revealed a disturbing narrative of deteriorating communication, escalating tensions, and finally, the ominous silence that signaled tragedy. The seemingly innocent digital trail, meticulously created by Gabby and Brian throughout their journey, became a key instrument in unraveling the events that led to Gabby's disappearance, highlighting the profound importance of digital evidence in modern criminal investigations. The seemingly mundane digital activities—a text message, a social media post, a GPS coordinate—took on immense significance when examined through the lens of time, place, and circumstance, helping to weave a narrative of a dream turned nightmare. This analysis highlighted the growing role of digital forensics in investigating complex crimes and underscored the importance of comprehensive data acquisition and analysis in unraveling even the most carefully constructed narratives of deception. The digital breadcrumb trail, though initially subtle and often fragmented, ultimately led investigators to the tragic truth.

Chapter Five

The Disappearance A Nations Attention

The initial days following Gabby's last contact were marked by a growing sense of unease among her family and friends. Nichole Schmidt, Gabby's mother, tried repeatedly to reach her daughter, the unanswered calls and texts escalating her anxiety into a full-blown panic. The idyllic van life adventure, so vibrantly documented on social media, had abruptly ended in silence. The cheerful posts and videos, previously a source of pride and joy, now felt like mocking reminders of a lost connection. This growing sense of dread propelled her into action, the initial hesitant inquiries to local law enforcement quickly transforming into a desperate plea for a full-scale investigation.

The lack of response from Brian Laundrie further fueled the apprehension. His return to Florida without Gabby, driving her van, was immediately suspicious. His silence, coupled with his refusal to cooperate with investigators, painted a picture of deliberate obfuscation, intensifying public scrutiny and prompting widespread speculation. The initial police reports, filed by Nichole Schmidt, meticulously documented the timeline of Gabby's last known contact, providing law enforcement with a critical starting point in the investigation. These reports, accessible to the public, fueled the burgeoning online interest in the case, transforming it from a local missing person's investigation into a national news story.

Social media, the same platform that had previously showcased Gabby and Brian's carefree travels, became the primary battleground for information dissemination and speculation. The hashtag #GabbyPetito rapidly gained traction, transforming the search effort into a collaborative endeavor between law enforcement, Gabby's family, and an army of online sleuths. These digital detectives, scouring through social media posts, analyzing metadata, and cross- referencing various sources of information, became critical players in the unfolding narrative. Their collective efforts, sometimes criticized for their amateur methods, ultimately helped to draw attention to the case and keep the pressure on law enforcement to act swiftly and decisively.

News outlets, both traditional and online, seized upon the story, feeding the public's insatiable appetite for updates. The case's captivating nature – a young couple on a dream road trip, ending in a tragic disappearance – resonated deeply with the public, drawing comparisons to other high-profile missing person cases. The constant media coverage, fueled by social media's rapid dissemination of information, ensured that Gabby's story remained at the forefront of public consciousness. The seemingly endless stream of news reports, analyses, and opinion pieces underscored the pervasive nature of the case and amplified the public's emotional investment in its resolution.

The narrative evolved in real-time, fueled by emerging information. Initial reports painted a picture of a missing person, gradually transforming into a full-blown murder investigation. This shift was driven not only by official pronouncements from law enforcement but also by the relentless digging of online investigators, who often unearthed details that were overlooked or initially disregarded. The collective effort of these individuals, however, wasn't without its drawbacks. Misinformation and unsubstantiated claims circulated alongside verifiable evidence, highlighting the complexities of navigating the digital landscape during a high-profile investigation. This constant influx of information, both accurate and inaccurate, made it challenging for law enforcement and the public alike to discern fact from speculation. The speed of dissemination often outpaced the ability of investigators to verify information, adding to the general atmosphere of urgency and uncertainty.

The involvement of online sleuths, though contributing to the public awareness of the case, also generated its own set of issues. The sheer volume of information, coupled with the lack of proper verification processes, led to the spread of unfounded rumors and unsubstantiated theories. Privacy concerns also arose as various social media profiles of Gabby, Brian, and their families were scrutinized, often without consent. The line between investigative journalism and online vigilantism blurred, raising ethical questions about the role of digital sleuths in high-profile investigations. The experience highlighted the need for responsible engagement in online investigations, with a strong emphasis on accuracy, verification, and respect for personal privacy.

The escalating media coverage created an unprecedented level of public pressure on law enforcement. Every development, every update, every press conference was meticulously scrutinized, analyzed, and dissected on social media platforms, news websites, and traditional news outlets. The demands for swift action, for transparent communication, and for answers were immense, reflecting the public's intense interest and investment in the case. This constant public scrutiny, while beneficial in some respects, could also place undue pressure on investigators, potentially hindering their ability to conduct a thorough and unbiased investigation.

The public outcry reflected a deeper societal concern about domestic violence and the potential for missed warning signs. The case brought the issue to the forefront of public discourse, sparking conversations about the prevalence of domestic abuse, the challenges faced by victims, and the need for better resources and support systems. The intense scrutiny placed on the details of Gabby and Brian's relationship, based on social media posts and witness testimonies, helped raise awareness of the subtle signs that might indicate a dangerous or abusive situation. The case sparked calls for improved education and awareness programs regarding domestic violence, highlighting the need for early intervention and preventative measures.

Gabby Petito's disappearance transformed from a personal tragedy into a national phenomenon, a testament to the power of social media in amplifying stories and mobilizing public support. The intense media scrutiny, coupled with the tireless efforts of online sleuths, played a crucial role in keeping the case in the public eye, generating pressure on law enforcement, and ultimately contributing to the investigation's outcome. However, the experience also served as a stark reminder of the challenges associated with navigating the ever-evolving landscape of online information, underscoring the need for responsible digital engagement and thoughtful consideration of the ethical implications of online investigations. The legacy of Gabby's story, far beyond the details of the case itself, lies in its powerful illustration of the potent interplay between technology, media, public perception, and the ongoing battle against domestic violence. Her story prompted crucial conversations about the need for better resources and support for victims of abuse, highlighting the importance of recognizing and addressing the subtle signs of danger within relationships. The national attention, while intense and sometimes overwhelming, ultimately helped to amplify the voices of those who had suffered in silence, contributing to a wider dialogue about violence, justice, and the complexities of human relationships in the digital age. The sheer volume of information, the rapid pace of the narrative's evolution, and the unprecedented levels of public involvement serve as a case study in the changing dynamics of news dissemination and the role of the public in modern criminal investigations. It also serves as a profound reminder of the fragility of life and the lasting impact a single tragedy can have on individuals, communities, and society as a whole.

Chapter Six

The Search for Gabby A MultiAgency Effort

The initial days of the search for Gabby Petito were marked by a frantic scramble, a multi-agency effort that rapidly expanded as the gravity of the situation became clear. The vastness of the search area, encompassing sprawling national parks and remote stretches of Wyoming, presented an immediate and significant challenge. The initial reports, filed by Gabby's mother, Nichole Schmidt, with the Suffolk County Police Department in New York, triggered the first steps in a complex jurisdictional dance. This initial contact set in motion a chain reaction, involving local, state, and eventually, federal agencies. The lack of concrete leads in the early stages forced investigators to cast a wide net, relying on fragmented information gleaned from Gabby and Brian's social media posts, their last known locations, and the sparse details provided by Brian Laundrie himself.

The Moab City Police Department in Utah, where Gabby and Brian had been involved in a domestic dispute prior to her disappearance, played a crucial early role. Their initial encounter with the couple, documented in a body camera video that later became a point of intense public scrutiny, provided a crucial glimpse into their relationship dynamics. While the police at the time chose not to file charges, opting instead for a temporary separation, the incident became a focal point in the subsequent investigation, raising questions about potential missed opportunities for intervention and the handling of domestic violence cases. The Moab police's involvement, initially limited to the domestic incident, expanded as the investigation progressed, with officers assisting in the broader search efforts and providing information to other agencies.

As the days turned into weeks, the search intensified. The National Park Service, responsible for the vast expanse of Grand Teton and Yellowstone National Parks, became heavily involved. Their expertise in wilderness search and rescue, coupled with their familiarity with the terrain, proved invaluable. Rangers, search and rescue teams, and park officials mobilized resources, deploying teams on foot, horseback, and using specialized equipment like drones and helicopters to comb through the rugged landscapes. Their efforts were hampered by the sheer scale of the search area, the unpredictable weather conditions, and the lack of readily apparent clues.

The FBI, bringing their extensive investigative resources and expertise to bear, also joined the search. Their involvement broadened the scope of the investigation beyond state lines, facilitating collaboration between different agencies and bringing a level of national attention and resources to the case. The FBI's expertise in digital forensics became critical, as investigators meticulously examined Gabby and Brian's phones, laptops, and social media accounts for any clues that might shed light on their movements and the circumstances surrounding Gabby's disappearance. This digital investigation would eventually prove pivotal in reconstructing the timeline of events and establishing a timeline leading up to Gabby's tragic end.

The coordination between the various agencies involved wasn't always seamless. The jurisdictional complexities, the sheer volume of information flowing in from various sources, and the pressure of intense public scrutiny presented significant challenges. Differing investigative approaches and communication gaps sometimes hampered the efficiency of the overall effort. The initial reports highlight some miscommunication between agencies in sharing information, delaying critical aspects of the search. However, as the urgency of the situation became apparent, the need for greater collaboration became paramount. Communication channels improved, information sharing became more streamlined, and a more unified approach to the investigation began to emerge.

Accounts from search and rescue teams involved paint a vivid picture of the grueling conditions they faced. The vastness of the wilderness, the unpredictable weather, and the challenging terrain all contributed to the difficulty of the search. Teams spent long hours hiking through rugged landscapes, often facing challenging weather conditions, tirelessly covering ground in the hope of finding any trace of Gabby. Their dedication and persistence, despite the exhaustion and lack of immediate results, were crucial to the overall investigation. They shared stories of navigating treacherous terrain, coping with exhaustion, and the emotional toll of searching for a missing person in such challenging conditions.

The investigation's timeline became a crucial piece of the puzzle. Investigators meticulously pieced together Gabby and Brian's movements using a combination of cell phone data, credit card records, social media activity, and witness accounts. This painstaking process was crucial in determining their likely route, pinpointing potential locations where Gabby might have been last seen, and providing search teams with key areas to focus their efforts. Mapping this timeline, charting their locations, became an integral part of the overall strategy, providing a visual representation of their journey and identifying gaps or discrepancies in their reported movements. The use of maps and timelines allowed investigators to visualize the scope of the search area, identify potential areas of interest, and prioritize their search efforts accordingly.

The search itself involved a diverse array of techniques and technologies. Traditional search methods, like ground searches and horseback patrols, were combined with more advanced technologies, such as aerial searches utilizing helicopters and drones equipped with thermal imaging capabilities. These technologies played a crucial role in covering vast areas quickly and efficiently, while simultaneously allowing investigators to focus their efforts on specific areas of interest identified through the timeline analysis. The use of drones, for example, allowed for the exploration of otherwise inaccessible areas, significantly expanding the scope of the search.

The involvement of K-9 units proved especially vital. Highly trained dogs, specialized in detecting human remains, were deployed to assist in the search, covering ground that might have otherwise been missed. Their keen sense of smell and ability to track faint scents were critical in identifying areas of potential interest, ultimately leading investigators to the location where Gabby's remains were eventually discovered. The canine units played a critical supporting role in the investigation, often providing vital clues that pointed investigators in the right direction.

The efforts involved in the search for Gabby Petito highlight the complex challenges involved in large-scale missing person investigations. The collaboration between numerous agencies, the diverse techniques employed, and the determination of the search teams all played a critical role in the eventual discovery of Gabby's remains. The case also served as a potent illustration of the critical importance of inter-agency cooperation and efficient communication in bringing a successful resolution to these types of investigations. The lessons learned from the challenges faced during the search have undoubtedly informed subsequent missing person cases, emphasizing the importance of early intervention, effective resource allocation, and the crucial role of technology in modern law enforcement. The experience underscored the need for comprehensive training in handling domestic violence cases, for improved coordination among agencies, and for the continued development of advanced search and rescue techniques. The enduring impact of Gabby's story remains not only in the tragic loss of a young life but also in the lessons learned and the lasting changes it prompted within the systems designed to prevent such tragedies from occurring again.

Chapter Seven

Brian Laundrie The Suspect Emerges

The spotlight, initially focused on the desperate search for Gabby Petito, inexorably shifted to Brian Laundrie. He transitioned from fiancé of a missing person to the prime suspect, a transformation fueled by his increasingly suspicious behavior and the mounting evidence against him. While the vast search for Gabby dominated headlines for weeks, a parallel investigation quietly intensified, its focus centered on Laundrie and the unraveling of his carefully constructed façade.

Laundrie's actions in the days following Gabby's last confirmed sighting spoke volumes, even before formal accusations were made. His return to his parents' Florida home without Gabby, his refusal to cooperate with investigators, and his subsequent lawyer's carefully worded statements all raised serious red flags. The initial public statements made by Laundrie's family offered little in the way of concrete information, only fueling speculation and increasing the pressure on law enforcement to act swiftly and decisively. This calculated silence, in the face of a nationwide search for Gabby, painted a picture of deliberate obfuscation, a tactic designed to hinder the investigation and create a buffer of uncertainty.

The silence was broken only after immense public pressure and the launch of a full-scale FBI investigation. The official statement from Laundrie's legal counsel was characterized by carefully chosen words and a staunch refusal to offer any substantial details regarding Gabby's whereabouts or the events leading up to her disappearance. The lawyer's strategy of non-cooperation became a significant part of the case's narrative, showcasing a calculated legal battle designed to protect Laundrie and potentially hinder the course of justice.

The timeline of Laundrie's activities after his return home became a key component of the investigative process. Investigators meticulously reconstructed his movements using a variety of sources, including credit card records, cell phone data, security footage, and witness statements. This reconstruction revealed a pattern of evasive behavior, with Laundrie taking steps to conceal his actions and avoid contact with authorities. The detail provided by witness accounts, often trivial in themselves, gradually formed a pattern suggesting a deliberate effort to remove traces of his involvement.

Financial records played a significant role in the investigation, offering insights into Laundrie's actions during the crucial period surrounding Gabby's disappearance. Investigators carefully examined credit card transactions and bank statements, seeking to map Laundrie's movements and identify any suspicious purchases or unusual financial activity. This meticulous review of his financial activity helped to establish a timeline of his actions, shedding light on possible locations he had visited and shedding light on the gaps in his accounts. Any discrepancies between Laundrie's claims and his financial records provided investigators with concrete evidence to pursue.

The investigation also delved into the digital footprint left behind by Laundrie. Investigators examined his phone, computer, and social media accounts, seeking digital clues that might reveal his involvement in Gabby's disappearance. The search for deleted files, hidden messages, and online activity related to the case proved crucial in piecing together a comprehensive picture of his activities during that critical time. The recovery of seemingly innocuous pieces of digital evidence often held unexpected significance and significance when considered within the larger context of the investigation. The digital forensics aspect of the case highlighted the increasing importance of digital evidence in contemporary criminal investigations.

A critical part of the investigation involved interviewing individuals who had interacted with Laundrie before and after Gabby's disappearance. Friends, family members, neighbors, and colleagues were interviewed to gather information about his behavior, his state of mind, and any potential clues that might shed light on his involvement in Gabby's disappearance. These interviews, often conducted separately, helped investigators piece together a narrative of Laundrie's actions in the days and weeks leading up to Gabby's death. Inconsistencies in the testimonies further helped investigators determine the level of Laundrie's deception.

One crucial aspect of the investigation was examining the nature of Laundrie's relationship with Gabby. Although they presented a seemingly idyllic image on social media, accounts from friends and family, along with police reports from earlier incidents, suggested a more complex and potentially volatile dynamic. Reports of arguments and disagreements, perhaps seemingly insignificant on their own, took on added significance within the context of Gabby's disappearance. The seemingly idyllic image on social media was carefully dissected by investigators to determine the real nature of the relationship. While the public initially perceived a happy couple, a fuller picture revealed a potentially troubled relationship, adding another layer to the unfolding narrative.

Witness testimonies provided a crucial piece of the puzzle. While many witnesses reported only fleeting interactions with the couple, their collective accounts contributed to a more detailed picture of Laundrie's behavior and movements. Some witnesses reported noticing Laundrie behaving suspiciously, while others provided details about his appearance or demeanor. Each piece of information, however small, was carefully analyzed and cross-referenced with other evidence to verify its reliability and its place within the broader investigative timeline. The accumulation of minor details painted a revealing portrait, demonstrating the power of collaborative investigation.

As the investigation progressed, the evidence pointing towards Laundrie's involvement grew more compelling. The lack of cooperation, his evasive actions, and the discrepancies between his statements and the available evidence created a strong circumstantial case against him. While direct evidence of his culpability was initially lacking, the cumulative weight of circumstantial evidence painted a damning portrait of a man involved in a tragic and devastating crime. The investigation's focus shifted from finding a missing person to bringing a suspected murderer to justice.

The intense media scrutiny surrounding the case added another layer of complexity to the investigation. The public's fervent interest in the case, fueled by the viral nature of Gabby's story and the tantalizing mystery surrounding Laundrie's actions, created an unprecedented level of public pressure on law enforcement. This pressure, while helpful in some respects, also presented potential challenges to the integrity of the investigation. The media's relentless pursuit of information and their often speculative reporting raised ethical considerations and potential risks to the overall process of bringing Laundrie to justice.

The case of Gabby Petito and Brian Laundrie stands as a chilling example of a domestic violence case spiraling into tragedy. It serves as a cautionary tale, underscoring the importance of early intervention, the need for improved communication and collaboration between law enforcement agencies, and the crucial role of digital forensics in modern criminal investigations. The case also highlights the immense power of social media in amplifying public attention and driving the investigation forward, albeit with potential risks and ethical considerations. The long and intricate investigation, filled with twists and turns, ultimately led to answers but also left many unanswered questions, serving as a reminder of the complexities and challenges inherent in solving even seemingly straightforward crimes. The comprehensive investigation into Laundrie's actions served as a case study in forensic investigation and the careful collection and analysis of circumstantial evidence. The eventual outcome, though tragic, served as a testament to the tireless dedication of law enforcement professionals in pursuing justice, even in the face of overwhelming public scrutiny and complex circumstances.

Chapter Eight

Forensic Evidence The Physical Clues

The discovery of Gabby Petito's remains in Grand Teton National Park marked a pivotal moment, shifting the investigation from a missing person case to a homicide investigation. The subsequent forensic examination of her body and the surrounding area became paramount in piecing together the final moments of her life and establishing the circumstances of her death. The autopsy report, a crucial piece of forensic evidence, detailed the cause and manner of death, providing investigators with a critical foundation for their investigation. While the specific details of the autopsy findings are often sealed due to the sensitive nature of the information, the report undoubtedly played a crucial role in guiding the direction of the investigation, informing subsequent investigative steps, and ultimately shaping the prosecution's case. The manner of death, confirmed through the autopsy, established the homicide, setting the stage for the extensive forensic investigation that followed.

The crime scene itself, encompassing the area where Gabby's body was discovered, underwent meticulous examination by forensic specialists. This included a thorough search for potential evidence, such as trace evidence, biological material, or any items that could link the scene to Brian Laundrie or shed light on the events leading up to Gabby's death. The analysis of the immediate surroundings, including the vegetation, soil, and any potential signs of a struggle, offered invaluable insights into the circumstances of Gabby's demise. Highly trained forensic scientists meticulously documented the scene, meticulously photographing and collecting evidence. The use of advanced technologies such as ground-penetrating radar and 3D scanning provided investigators with a comprehensive record of the location and a detailed visual representation of the crime scene. This digital documentation helped to reconstruct the events, making the scene "speak" even after the physical evidence was removed for laboratory analysis.

Beyond the immediate vicinity of Gabby's remains, investigators broadened their search to include locations identified through the investigation's timeline. This included the couple's travel route, documented through social media posts, credit card transactions, and cell phone data. The search for physical evidence expanded to campsites, rest stops, and other locations where Gabby and Brian had been sighted. Any items discovered at these locations, even seemingly insignificant ones, were meticulously collected and analyzed in the forensic laboratory to assess their potential relevance to the case. This painstaking process, often described as the "search for the needle in the haystack," is a hallmark of modern forensic investigations. The investigators' commitment to thoroughness was crucial in bringing together the fragmented pieces of evidence to paint a fuller picture.

Forensic analysis went beyond the physical crime scene. The van, a significant element in the couple's cross-country trip, became a critical piece of evidence. The van underwent a thorough examination to identify any physical traces that might connect Brian Laundrie to Gabby's death or provide insights into the events leading up to it. Investigators meticulously searched for any biological evidence such as blood, hair, or fibers; they also looked for signs of a struggle or any evidence that indicated a violent altercation. The van's interior was carefully documented, photographed, and analyzed for any trace evidence that might provide crucial details about what happened. The examination extended to the van's exterior, searching for traces of soil, debris, or other material that might link the van to specific locations along the couple's route.

Digital forensics played a crucial, and often underappreciated, role in this investigation. The examination of Brian Laundrie's electronic devices – his phone, computer, and any other digital devices he possessed – provided invaluable insights into his activities and mindset in the days and weeks leading up to Gabby's disappearance. The recovery of deleted data, including text messages, emails, photos, and internet browsing history, provided valuable information, even if some data required specialized techniques to recover. Data recovery specialists used sophisticated software to recover deleted files and reconstruct the digital timeline. Any inconsistencies between his digital footprint and his statements to investigators provided crucial evidence to fuel the investigation.

Social media posts, seemingly innocuous on their surface, also became crucial pieces of digital evidence when analyzed within the context of the investigation. Photographs and videos, carefully scrutinized by investigators, offered clues about their movements, their state of mind, and any potential conflicts within their relationship. Investigators often employed image analysis and geolocation technology to pinpoint exact locations and verify the claims made by Brian Laundrie. The meticulous examination of seemingly minor details in the social media posts helped investigators build a timeline of events, identify discrepancies, and ultimately gather evidence to corroborate witness testimonies and other forms of forensic evidence. The power of social media, initially celebrated for its potential to assist in the search, also played a significant role in providing investigators with vital information to aid their forensic inquiries.

The analysis of Brian Laundrie's financial records – credit card transactions, bank statements, and any other financial documents – offered crucial details regarding his movements and activities after Gabby's disappearance. Investigators used financial records to trace his spending patterns, identify locations he had visited, and verify his claims regarding his whereabouts. Discrepancies between his financial records and his stated activities played a significant role in establishing a more accurate timeline of events and challenging his claims of innocence. Such financial evidence is often crucial in cases of this type, and provided investigators with concrete evidence to pursue, helping to piece together the puzzle of his actions.

The integration of all forms of forensic evidence – the autopsy report, crime scene analysis, examination of the van, digital forensics, and financial records – proved vital in building a comprehensive understanding of the events surrounding Gabby Petito's death. The meticulous collection and analysis of these diverse pieces of evidence, combined with witness testimonies and investigative work, enabled investigators to reconstruct a detailed timeline of events, ultimately supporting the conclusion of Brian Laundrie's culpability. The case stands as a clear demonstration of the crucial role that forensic science plays in modern criminal investigations, showcasing the ability of forensic techniques to uncover crucial evidence, even in seemingly complicated circumstances. The integration of various forensic disciplines allowed for a holistic approach to the investigation, providing a powerful narrative that contributed to the resolution of the case, despite its tragic outcome. The details of the forensic evidence, while often complex, underscore the value of meticulous, scientific investigation in bringing justice to victims and holding those responsible accountable.

Chapter Nine

Digital Forensics The Online Trail

The digital realm offered a parallel investigation, a silent witness to the unfolding drama. Gabby and Brian's digital footprints, initially seemingly innocuous snapshots of their van life adventure, became crucial pieces of the puzzle, offering a glimpse into their relationship dynamics and the events preceding Gabby's tragic death. The investigation's digital forensics team faced a monumental task: recovering and analyzing data from multiple devices, potentially damaged or deliberately destroyed, scattered across different jurisdictions and time zones.

The first challenge was securing and preserving the digital evidence. Brian Laundrie's personal devices—his phone, laptop, and potentially other electronic gadgets—were critical targets. Law enforcement had to act swiftly to prevent data loss or alteration, employing specialized techniques to create forensic copies of the devices' contents without compromising the original evidence. This involved sophisticated hardware and software capable of imaging hard drives, extracting data from memory chips, and recovering deleted files, a process that required specialized expertise and meticulous attention to detail. Even seemingly insignificant devices, such as a digital camera or a smartwatch, could yield valuable information. The process wasn't simply about copying data; it involved adhering to strict chain-of-custody protocols, meticulously documenting every step of the process to ensure the admissibility of the evidence in court. Any breach in this procedure could jeopardize the entire digital investigation.

Once secured, the data extraction began. This wasn't a simple matter of browsing through photos and text messages. Specialized software was used to dissect the devices' contents, recovering deleted files, fragments of data, and metadata—information about the data itself, such as creation dates, modification times, and location data. This often involved sifting through terabytes of data, a painstaking process requiring powerful computers and sophisticated algorithms. The investigators focused on recovering deleted content, as this often holds vital clues. People often delete incriminating evidence, believing it is gone forever, but digital forensics can often recover it. The recovery of deleted text messages, emails, photos, and internet browsing history were particularly valuable in piecing together the timeline and understanding the couple's interactions.

The analysis of Gabby's phone was equally vital, though her device may have held less incriminating information. However, it could provide valuable context, such as the last messages she sent, the location data embedded in her photos, and any communication she had with Brian or others. By cross-referencing her phone data with Brian's, investigators could identify inconsistencies, corroborate witness testimonies, and potentially uncover evidence of conflict or abuse. The examination of GPS data, metadata from photos and videos, and other location-based information provided critical clues about their movements. This allowed investigators to reconstruct their travel route, pinpoint potential crime scenes, and corroborate witness accounts.

Social media presented a unique challenge and opportunity. Gabby and Brian's social media profiles, filled with seemingly idyllic snapshots of their cross-country trip, offered a different perspective when analyzed meticulously. Investigators scoured their posts, photos, and videos, not only for overt clues but also for subtle hints, inconsistencies, or changes in their behavior. The photos were geolocated, verifying their claims about their locations and revealing potential discrepancies. The investigators even utilized facial recognition software to analyze the emotional expressions in the photographs and videos, searching for signs of stress, anxiety, or even fear. The tone and content of their posts were scrutinized for changes or indications of conflict. Even seemingly insignificant details, like the date and time of the posts and the specific locations tagged, were carefully considered.

The digital forensics team also looked beyond the obvious. They examined the metadata associated with images and videos, searching for details like the date, time, and location of creation. This information could be more accurate than the timestamp on a social media post, allowing investigators to create a more precise timeline. The team also investigated deleted content from their social media accounts. This was often where people hid or deleted evidence they felt was incriminating. The recovery of deleted messages and posts could reveal important details about their relationship and the events surrounding Gabby's disappearance.

One significant aspect of the investigation was the analysis of metadata related to location. Cell tower data, GPS information embedded in photos and videos, and location services enabled investigators to track their movements across the country, verifying their claims and revealing any deviations from their declared itinerary. Discrepancies between their stated location and their actual location based on the device data provided critical investigative leads. By overlaying this location data onto maps, the investigators created a visual timeline of their travels, highlighting potential stops, encounters, and areas of interest. This was particularly helpful in narrowing down the search for Gabby's remains.

Another challenge for the digital forensics team was the vastness of the data. The sheer volume of information extracted from the devices and social media accounts required sophisticated analytical tools and significant manpower. The data required meticulous organization and categorization before any meaningful analysis could take place. Advanced search techniques and data visualization tools were utilized to sift through the data, searching for specific keywords, patterns, and anomalies. The collaboration of multiple experts—digital forensics specialists, data analysts, and investigators—was vital to ensure the efficient and thorough examination of the evidence. The findings were then meticulously documented and presented to the investigation team, forming a crucial component of the overall case.

The analysis of digital evidence uncovered numerous important pieces of information. Text messages might reveal heated arguments, subtle signs of control, or plans indicating malice. Emails could uncover hidden communication channels or financial transactions. Internet browsing history could reveal searches relating to violence, self-harm, or methods of concealment. These seemingly disparate pieces of information, when pieced together, could form a comprehensive picture of the events leading up to Gabby's disappearance and death. The digital evidence played a pivotal role in establishing a timeline, corroborating witness testimonies, and ultimately leading to Brian Laundrie's prosecution, underscoring the increasing importance of digital forensics in modern criminal investigations. The digital trail, initially appearing fragmented and scattered, ultimately became a crucial pathway to unraveling the truth behind Gabby Petito's disappearance and death.

Chapter Ten

The Discovery of Gabby's Remains A Grim Confirmation

The weeks following Gabby Petito's disappearance stretched into an agonizing eternity, a period punctuated by frantic searches, fervent social media pleas, and a mounting sense of dread. The national spotlight, initially focused on the missing young woman and her fiancé's unsettling silence, intensified with each passing day. Every lead, however tenuous, was relentlessly pursued, every potential sighting investigated with painstaking detail. The vast expanse of Grand Teton National Park, with its rugged terrain and sprawling wilderness, presented an immense challenge to search and rescue teams. Days bled into weeks, hope slowly ebbing away with each fruitless search.

Then, on September 19th, 2021, the news broke that shattered the fragile optimism that had stubbornly persisted. Gabby Petito's remains had been discovered at a campsite in Bridger-Teton National Forest in Wyoming, not far from where she and Brian Laundrie had last been seen together. The announcement, delivered with a somber gravity by law enforcement officials, sent shockwaves across the nation. The once-vibrant image of a young woman embarking on a dream cross-country adventure was irrevocably replaced by the stark reality of a tragic and untimely death.

The discovery of Gabby's body marked a pivotal moment in the investigation, shifting the focus from a missing person case to a homicide inquiry. The location of the remains, close to where the couple had been camping, strongly suggested that the crime scene lay within the national forest. This immediately concentrated law enforcement efforts on a more defined area, facilitating a more focused and thorough search for additional evidence, including potential weapons or other clues related to the crime. The investigation, already massive in scope, now required even greater coordination and resources. Specialized teams were deployed to the site, meticulously documenting the scene, collecting evidence, and conducting a thorough forensic examination.

The ensuing autopsy, conducted by the Teton County Coroner's Office, confirmed the worst fears. Gabby Petito had died from blunt force injuries to the head and neck, consistent with manual strangulation. The manner of death was ruled a homicide. The report, released later, provided further details, including the specific injuries sustained and the estimated time of death, offering invaluable insights into the circumstances surrounding her demise. This confirmation tragically brought an end to the agonizing uncertainty that had gripped Gabby's family, friends, and the millions who had followed her story. The details released by the coroner's office, while devastating, provided a crucial foundation for the ongoing criminal investigation.

The official confirmation of Gabby's death ignited a wave of grief and outrage across the nation. The outpouring of public sympathy for her family was immense, reflecting a collective sense of loss and a visceral reaction to the senseless violence that had ended her life. The story had captivated the nation, turning Gabby into a symbol of the dangers faced by women, particularly those involved in relationships characterized by potential abuse. Social media, which had initially played a pivotal role in spreading awareness about Gabby's disappearance, now became a platform for expressing condolences, sharing memories, and demanding justice. The hashtags #JusticeForGabby and #FindGabby, which had initially driven the search efforts, now became rallying cries for accountability and an end to domestic violence.

The public's reaction was far from uniform. While the majority expressed sorrow and anger at Gabby's death and called for justice, some voices emerged expressing skepticism about the details of the case, spreading misinformation, and even resorting to harassment of individuals involved. The intense scrutiny surrounding the investigation and the public's intense emotional investment in the case presented both opportunities and challenges to law enforcement and the investigative team. The pressure to solve the case quickly and effectively was immense, placing immense pressure on investigators. The desire for justice had to be balanced with the need for a thorough and impartial investigation. The vast amount of digital evidence and the proliferation of speculation on social media presented an unprecedented challenge, requiring sophisticated analysis and careful verification of facts.

The emotional toll on Gabby's family was immeasurable. The discovery of her remains confirmed their worst nightmare, ending weeks of agonizing uncertainty and plunging them into unimaginable grief. Their public statements, characterized by both sorrow and determination, underscored the impact of their loss and their unwavering resolve to seek justice for their daughter. The media's coverage of their statements and their grief resonated deeply with the public, reinforcing the emotional weight of the tragedy. The family's strength and resilience in the face of such overwhelming sorrow provided both inspiration and a stark reminder of the devastating consequences of violence against women.

The investigation, however, did not end with the discovery of Gabby's body. The focus now shifted to Brian Laundrie, her fiancé, who had returned home from their trip without her and had subsequently refused to cooperate with investigators. The autopsy findings and the timeline constructed from digital evidence and witness statements provided critical clues in pointing towards Laundrie as the prime suspect in Gabby's murder. The discovery of Gabby's remains marked a significant turning point in the investigation, accelerating the efforts to locate and apprehend Brian Laundrie and bring him to justice. The timeline, painstakingly pieced together from various sources, including cell phone records, credit card transactions, and witness testimonies, helped investigators trace their movements in the days and weeks leading up to Gabby's disappearance and death.

The evidence, meticulously gathered and analyzed, pointed toward a deteriorating relationship marked by escalating conflicts. This timeline, corroborated by digital evidence recovered from both Gabby and Brian's devices, painted a disturbing picture of the events that ultimately led to Gabby's death. The forensic analysis of Gabby's remains, coupled with the digital evidence and witness testimonies, provided investigators with a robust case against Brian Laundrie. The digital trail, initially seemingly innocuous, had revealed crucial details, shedding light on the events leading up to her death and strengthening the evidence against the prime suspect. The investigation, far from ending with the discovery of Gabby's remains, had just entered a new and equally critical phase. The hunt for Brian Laundrie and the subsequent legal proceedings would be just as closely followed and analyzed by the public. The tragic death of Gabby Petito served as a stark reminder of the urgent need to address domestic violence, to improve resources for victims, and to ensure that no one else suffers the same fate. The national conversation sparked by her death continues, prompting calls for improved laws, increased support systems, and a greater societal awareness of the pervasive problem of domestic abuse.

Chapter Eleven

The Power of Social Media A Double Edged Sword

The immediacy and reach of social media transformed the Gabby Petito case from a local investigation into a national, and arguably international, phenomenon. Within hours of the initial missing person report, the news spread like wildfire across platforms like Facebook, Twitter, Instagram, and TikTok. Gabby's vibrant travel vlogs, previously shared for the enjoyment of friends and family, became crucial pieces of evidence, meticulously dissected by online communities. These videos, initially showcasing a seemingly idyllic cross- country adventure, were now viewed with a chilling new perspective, their lighthearted tone starkly juxtaposed with the unfolding tragedy. Each frame, each subtle expression, was scrutinized for clues, fueling an insatiable public appetite for information.

The sheer volume of information circulating online was unprecedented. Official statements from law enforcement were interwoven with amateur speculation, eyewitness accounts, and conspiracy theories. The lack of readily available, verified information from official channels created a vacuum quickly filled by the relentless churn of social media. This created both advantages and significant drawbacks to the investigative process.

On one hand, social media became an invaluable tool for disseminating information. The widespread sharing of Gabby's image and details helped propel the case into the national spotlight, attracting attention from law enforcement agencies, media outlets, and volunteer search parties. The hashtags #JusticeForGabby and #FindGabby mobilized a vast network of online users who actively shared information, analyzed clues, and provided crucial leads to investigators.

The power of collective online action cannot be underestimated; it amplified the search efforts and kept public pressure on law enforcement to act swiftly and decisively. This digital amplification, while potentially chaotic, was instrumental in transforming a missing person case into a national priority.

The role of "digital sleuths" deserves particular attention. These online investigators, armed with a mixture of technical expertise, investigative curiosity, and often considerable free time, poured over publicly available information, scrutinizing social media posts, mapping GPS coordinates, and analyzing forensic evidence. Some contributed significantly, providing investigators with leads that might otherwise have been missed. They identified inconsistencies in Brian Laundrie's statements, tracked the couple's movements using social media posts and geotagging data, and pieced together a timeline that assisted law enforcement in their investigation. Their efforts, often conducted collaboratively across different platforms, highlighted the potential of citizen involvement in investigations.

However, the contributions of digital sleuths were not always beneficial. The speed and scale of online information sharing also led to the rapid spread of misinformation and speculation. Unverified claims, rumors, and outright false information quickly proliferated, often overshadowing factual updates from official sources. The constant barrage of unconfirmed details and contradictory narratives muddied the waters, complicating the investigative process and creating unnecessary distress for Gabby's family. This uncontrolled dissemination of potentially inaccurate information hampered the efforts of law enforcement.

The emotional intensity fueled by social media also presented ethical challenges. Online discussions often veered into hostile territory, with users directing harassment and abuse at Brian Laundrie, his family, and even those perceived to be sympathetic to the Laundrie family. The intense scrutiny, amplified by social media's echo chambers, created an environment of emotional volatility and potential for misdirected anger. This online harassment was not only distressing for those targeted but also risked compromising the integrity of the investigation by potentially influencing witnesses or creating a climate of fear.

The speed at which this case evolved online was also unprecedented. The 24/7 news cycle, amplified by social media's real-time nature, created intense pressure on law enforcement to provide regular updates. This demand, fueled by the constant barrage of online speculation and commentary, inevitably led to both frustration and potentially premature information releases. Maintaining the integrity of the investigation while managing public expectations in this highly charged environment proved extraordinarily challenging. The constant need to respond to online speculation risked compromising the investigative process and inadvertently releasing information that could have hampered the legal proceedings.

The deluge of images, videos, and commentary also created a challenge for the media landscape. Traditional news outlets struggled to keep up with the sheer volume of information circulating online, leading to a sometimes chaotic and disjointed reporting process. The need to verify information and maintain journalistic integrity was often overshadowed by the relentless pace of online developments. This blurred the lines between responsible reporting and the often unchecked spread of speculation, creating a climate where truth and falsehood became increasingly difficult to discern. The resulting media frenzy further amplified the intense pressure on law enforcement and the families involved.

Furthermore, the case highlighted the inherent biases embedded within social media algorithms and the echo chambers they create. Users' pre-existing beliefs and biases influenced the information they consumed and shared, reinforcing existing narratives and often amplifying already polarized viewpoints. The algorithmic amplification of specific narratives, irrespective of their factual accuracy, further contributed to the spread of misinformation and the polarization of opinions surrounding the case. The sheer volume of content, coupled with the selective algorithms that shaped users' feeds, prevented a balanced understanding of the case for many online users.

Ultimately, the Gabby Petito case serves as a powerful illustration of social media's dual nature as both a tool for good and a breeding ground for misinformation and online harassment. While social media helped amplify the search for Gabby and brought attention to the tragic circumstances of her disappearance, its use also exacerbated existing anxieties and fueled a media frenzy that created significant challenges for the investigative process and those directly impacted by the case. The lessons learned from this experience highlight the urgent need for greater media literacy and improved strategies for managing the spread of misinformation in the context of high-profile criminal investigations. This case underscores the importance of balancing the potential benefits of online participation in investigations with the undeniable risks associated with unchecked speculation, harassment, and the spread of false narratives. The enduring legacy of this case extends beyond the tragic loss of Gabby Petito; it serves as a critical examination of the evolving relationship between social media, criminal investigations, and public perception. The complex dynamics of the case serve as a case study for how to navigate the challenges of online information sharing in the age of social media, a lesson for law enforcement, the media, and the public alike. The ongoing debate about the appropriate role of social media in criminal investigations will undoubtedly continue, shaped by the lessons learned from the Gabby Petito case.

Chapter Twelve

The News Cycle Sensationalism vs Responsibility

The relentless 24/7 news cycle, amplified by the insatiable appetite of social media, transformed the Gabby Petito case into a media spectacle of unprecedented proportions. The line between responsible journalism and sensationalism blurred, creating a complex and often troubling landscape of information dissemination. While the media played a crucial role in raising awareness and generating public pressure to find Gabby, the sheer volume of coverage, coupled with the often-unverified nature of online reports, cast a long shadow over the investigation and its participants.

The initial reports were understandably focused on the missing person aspect. Gabby's image, drawn from her vibrant travel vlogs, became instantly recognizable, her bright smile a stark contrast to the growing anxiety surrounding her disappearance. News outlets, both traditional and online, scrambled to provide updates, often relying on information gleaned from social media and unconfirmed sources. This early phase saw a commendable effort to keep the public informed, but it also laid the groundwork for the intense media frenzy that followed.

As the investigation progressed and more details emerged, the focus shifted. The narrative increasingly centered on Brian Laundrie, initially a person of interest, then a suspect. The media's portrayal of Laundrie evolved from that of a concerned fiancé to a prime suspect, a shift fueled by speculation and the release of fragmented pieces of information. The public's attention turned to the Laundrie family, their silence and perceived lack of cooperation becoming targets of intense scrutiny and, in many cases, online harassment. The relentless media coverage contributed to the creation of an atmosphere of suspicion and distrust, impacting the lives of those who had nothing to do with Gabby's disappearance.

The ethical considerations of reporting on such a sensitive case were often overlooked in the rush to break the next story. The intense public interest created a pressure cooker environment where accuracy and sensitivity were often sacrificed for speed and sensationalism. Examples of irresponsible reporting abounded. Some news outlets jumped to conclusions based on limited evidence, while others focused heavily on the more sensational aspects of the case, such as the details of Gabby and Brian's relationship or the specifics of the couple's travel plans. This approach not only risked prejudicing potential jurors but also created an environment where speculation and conspiracy theories could flourish, further hindering the investigation.

In contrast, some news organizations demonstrated a commendable commitment to responsible reporting. These outlets prioritized fact-checking and verification, carefully scrutinizing information before publishing it. They approached the story with sensitivity, acknowledging the emotional toll on Gabby's family and refraining from gratuitous exploitation of the tragedy. They understood that their role extended beyond simply reporting facts; it included considering the impact of their reporting on the victims, their families, and the broader community. The stark contrast between responsible and irresponsible reporting highlighted the crucial role that journalistic ethics played in navigating this highly charged situation.

The media's portrayal of Gabby herself deserves specific attention. While many outlets presented her as a vibrant, adventurous young woman, some fell into the trap of victim- blaming, focusing on aspects of her personality or behavior that were entirely irrelevant to the core issue: a violent crime. This approach not only undermined the gravity of the situation but also risked perpetuating harmful stereotypes about domestic violence victims. The media had a responsibility to present a nuanced and accurate portrayal of Gabby, highlighting her positive qualities while acknowledging the complexities of her relationship with Brian. This responsibility was not always met.

The media's influence extended beyond simply shaping the narrative; it had a profound impact on public opinion. The constant stream of news reports, coupled with the deluge of online commentary, created a polarized public sphere where opinions ranged from intense sympathy for Gabby to suspicion, and even animosity, towards Brian and his family. Social media, in particular, became a breeding ground for speculation, misinformation, and often vicious online harassment. This environment made it difficult to discern truth from fiction, further complicating the situation for investigators and the families involved.

The impact on Gabby's family cannot be overstated. The media frenzy subjected them to an unbearable level of scrutiny and intrusion. Their grief was compounded by the constant barrage of attention, the pressure to speak to the media, and the emotional toll of navigating the complexities of a high-profile investigation. The constant need to respond to media inquiries and deal with the relentless public attention added layers of stress and trauma to their already unimaginable suffering.

Furthermore, the case exposed the limitations of traditional media in keeping pace with the rapid dissemination of information in the digital age. The constant flow of information on social media, often unverified and contradictory, challenged the traditional journalistic process of verification and fact-checking. The media's struggle to keep pace with this rapid flow of information further highlighted the challenges of providing accurate and timely coverage in the context of a constantly evolving news cycle.

The Gabby Petito case serves as a cautionary tale about the power of the media and the importance of responsible reporting. While the media played a vital role in raising awareness and keeping public pressure on law enforcement, it also demonstrated the potential for sensationalism to overshadow ethical considerations and compromise the integrity of the investigation. The case highlights the need for greater media literacy among the public, a renewed commitment to ethical journalism, and a clearer understanding of the complexities of reporting on sensitive criminal investigations in the digital age. The long-term consequences of the media frenzy, both for the families involved and for the broader public understanding of the case, underscore the need for a critical examination of the media's role in shaping public perception and influencing the course of justice. The lessons learned from this tragedy should serve as a guide for future coverage of high-profile criminal investigations. The pursuit of truth should always supersede the pursuit of sensational headlines.

Chapter Thirteen

The Role of Online Communities Support and Speculation

The digital age, with its instantaneous communication and vast interconnectedness, fostered the rapid growth of online communities surrounding Gabby Petito's disappearance. These virtual spaces, born from the collective grief and shared desire for justice, quickly evolved into complex ecosystems of support, speculation, and, at times, outright toxicity. Initially, these online communities provided a crucial lifeline for Gabby's family and friends, offering a platform for sharing information, coordinating search efforts, and providing emotional support during an incredibly difficult time. Facebook groups, dedicated subreddits, and Twitter hashtags became hubs of activity, connecting people across geographical boundaries who were united in their concern for Gabby's well-being.

The sheer volume of information shared within these online communities was staggering. Family and friends posted updates on the investigation, shared photos and videos of Gabby, and appealed for anyone with information to come forward. These groups became vital tools for disseminating information that might otherwise have been missed by traditional media outlets. Users crowdsourced potential leads, meticulously analyzing social media posts, travel logs, and even satellite imagery to piece together a timeline of Gabby and Brian Laundrie's movements. The collective intelligence of these digital sleuths proved invaluable, accelerating the pace of the investigation in ways that traditional investigative methods might not have been able to achieve. Some users, leveraging their own technical skills, created interactive maps tracking the couple's journey, highlighting potential points of interest and possible locations where Gabby might have been last seen. This collaborative approach demonstrated the remarkable potential of online communities to assist in solving complex missing person cases. Their efforts provided law enforcement with valuable information and significantly expanded the scope of the search.

However, the inherent nature of online forums – their lack of centralized moderation and verification protocols – also contributed to the spread of misinformation and speculation. The absence of editorial oversight allowed rumors, unsubstantiated claims, and outright conspiracy theories to proliferate. Unverified images, videos, and documents circulated rapidly, creating a chaotic landscape of information where discerning fact from fiction became an increasingly difficult task. This environment fostered an atmosphere of distrust, not only towards law enforcement but also between users themselves. The lack of accountability allowed users to post potentially damaging information without fear of immediate consequences, often with devastating results. For example, some individuals mistakenly identified people who resembled Brian Laundrie, leading to public shaming and harassment of innocent individuals. Other users spread baseless accusations about the Laundrie family, subjecting them to a wave of online abuse and vitriol.

The emotional intensity surrounding Gabby's case magnified the negative aspects of online communities. The public's desperate yearning for answers fueled the spread of speculation, with many users drawing their own conclusions based on limited or incomplete evidence. This led to the creation of numerous conspiracy theories, ranging from theories of government cover-ups to unsubstantiated claims about Gabby's death. The rapid dissemination of these theories through social media created a toxic environment that undermined the integrity of the investigation and compounded the suffering of Gabby's family. The sheer volume of speculation made it increasingly challenging for law enforcement to sort through the deluge of information, identify credible leads, and maintain the focus necessary for a thorough investigation.

The anonymity afforded by many online platforms further exacerbated the problem. Users were able to post inflammatory comments and engage in harmful behavior without fear of being held accountable for their actions. This lack of accountability fueled the spread of hateful rhetoric and cyberbullying, creating a toxic online environment that threatened the mental health and well-being of individuals involved in the case, both directly and indirectly. The line between expressing concerns and engaging in harassment frequently blurred, resulting in attacks targeting not only Brian Laundrie, but also his family and even unrelated individuals who were mistakenly identified as being connected to the case.

The role of online influencers and social media personalities also warrants careful consideration. Some leveraged the tragedy to gain notoriety, capitalizing on the immense public interest to generate views and followers. This exploitation of Gabby's disappearance for personal gain fueled the negative aspects of online communities, contributing to a climate of sensationalism and irresponsible behavior. The rapid dissemination of their often-unverified information further exacerbated the spread of misinformation, hindering the efforts of law enforcement and adding to the emotional distress of those involved. The focus on likes, shares, and views often overshadowed the need for responsible reporting and accurate information.

Despite these significant drawbacks, it's important to acknowledge that online communities also offered a platform for organizing support and resource mobilization. Fundraising efforts to support

Gabby's family were launched and successfully managed through online platforms, demonstrating the power of these digital spaces to facilitate collective action and provide tangible assistance during a time of crisis. Many users contributed to funding the investigation and offered their support to Gabby's family. While the negative aspects of these online spaces were considerable, it's crucial to acknowledge the positive contributions some individuals made. The balance between the helpful and the harmful underscores the complex and often contradictory nature of online communities in the context of a high-profile tragedy like Gabby Petito's case.

The experience of the online communities surrounding Gabby Petito's case underscores the double-edged sword of the digital age. While these spaces offered unprecedented opportunities for information sharing, support, and collaboration, they also amplified the spread of misinformation, speculation, and online harassment. The lack of robust moderation and verification mechanisms in many online platforms allowed rumors and conspiracy theories to flourish, potentially undermining the investigation and harming individuals caught in the crossfire. The case highlights the need for greater media literacy, enhanced efforts to combat online misinformation, and increased responsibility amongst users and platform owners to create safer and more constructive online environments.

The experience of Gabby's case serves as a cautionary tale for future investigations, highlighting the importance of responsible digital citizenship and the need for a critical approach to information consumed online. The lessons learned from this tragedy can inform future efforts to balance the benefits of online collaboration with the need to mitigate the risks associated with unmoderated and unregulated online spaces. The enduring impact of the online reactions to Gabby Petito's case should prompt a broader societal discussion about the role of online communities in the age of instantaneous information, emphasizing the imperative for responsible engagement and the critical need for informed judgment. The potential for both harm and good remains immense, and the future depends on our ability to harness the positive aspects of these powerful digital tools while mitigating their inherent risks.

Chapter Fourteen

Public Outrage and the Demand for Justice

The discovery of Gabby Petito's body ignited a firestorm of public outrage, unlike anything seen in recent memory surrounding a missing person case. The initial wave of sympathy and concern for a young woman vanished on a cross-country road trip quickly escalated into a demand for justice, fueled by a potent cocktail of factors. The idyllic images of Gabby's van life adventures, meticulously documented and shared on social media, created a stark contrast to the grim reality of her tragic end. This juxtaposition amplified the sense of loss and injustice, leaving many feeling a profound sense of personal connection to the case. The seemingly effortless transition from vibrant social media posts depicting a carefree adventure to the chilling reality of a homicide deeply affected millions. The carefully curated online persona Gabby presented, juxtaposed against the horrifying reality of her demise, intensified public grief and outrage. This created a powerful emotional response from a vast audience who saw themselves reflected in her seemingly normal, aspirational journey.

The relentless media coverage, initially focused on finding Gabby, shifted to a critical examination of the investigation's progress (or lack thereof). The perceived slow pace of the official inquiry, coupled with the release of fragmented and often contradictory information, fueled speculation and distrust in law enforcement. The public scrutinized every official statement, every press conference, searching for signs of incompetence or worse, deliberate obstruction. The perception that law enforcement was not acting with sufficient urgency or effectiveness contributed significantly to the growing public frustration and the escalating demands for accountability. The contrasting speed of the online investigation, fueled by digital sleuths piecing together clues from social media posts and other online sources, further exacerbated these criticisms. The disparity between the speed of the online investigative efforts and the perceived slow response of law enforcement agencies only served to increase public anger.

The intense public scrutiny wasn't limited to the investigative agencies; it extended to Brian Laundrie, Gabby's fiancé and the primary person of interest in the case. The public, informed by the ever-increasing flow of information from various media outlets and online sources, formed its own narrative, largely fueled by social media's instantaneous and often unchecked dissemination of information. This often led to premature conclusions and judgments, with the result being an immense pressure mounted on law enforcement to act decisively, even as the investigation progressed. This intense public pressure, while demonstrating a collective desire for justice, also created a challenging environment for law enforcement to conduct a thorough and impartial investigation. The intense media scrutiny was largely amplified by the highly publicized nature of Gabby's social media presence prior to her disappearance, effectively catapulting the case to national prominence.

The case also triggered a broader societal reckoning with domestic violence and its insidious nature. While not initially a primary focus, as more information emerged, evidence of a strained relationship between Gabby and Brian emerged, highlighted by witness accounts, bodycam footage, and social media posts suggesting a pattern of conflict. The public began to connect the dots, piecing together a narrative of escalating tensions and possible abuse, resulting in a renewed focus on addressing the pervasive issue of domestic violence and the need for improved support systems for victims. The tragedy served as a stark reminder of the dangers faced by women in abusive relationships and highlighted the critical need for comprehensive awareness campaigns and improved legal protections.

The impact extended far beyond the specific details of the case. Gabby Petito's story transcended the boundaries of a single tragedy, becoming a symbol for a national conversation about missing persons, particularly missing women. The case raised important questions about the effectiveness of law enforcement responses to missing person reports, particularly those involving domestic violence. Critics argued that the initial responses to Gabby's disappearance were slow, complacent, and potentially hampered by systemic issues within law enforcement agencies. The case highlighted the need for improved protocols, better training, and a greater emphasis on prioritizing cases involving potential domestic violence. The disparity in media attention and investigative resources dedicated to different missing persons cases based on race and socioeconomic status was also a point of contention. Many argued that the overwhelming public attention and resources devoted to Gabby's case underscored an existing inequity in the justice system, with missing persons of color often receiving far less media coverage and investigative resources.

The public demand for justice manifested in various ways. Online petitions circulated, demanding increased accountability for law enforcement and greater resources for missing person investigations. Vigils and memorial events were held across the country, expressing collective grief and solidarity with Gabby's family. The case ignited broader conversations about the role of social media in solving crimes and the potential for both positive and negative impacts of the online sphere. While the swift spread of information online was credited with accelerating the search for Gabby and generating public pressure on law enforcement, it also fueled misinformation and speculation, highlighting the complex and often contradictory role of social media in criminal investigations.

The intense public reaction to Gabby Petito's case left an enduring legacy, extending beyond the immediate aftermath of her death. It prompted reviews of law enforcement procedures and training related to domestic violence and missing person cases. The case raised significant questions about the effectiveness of current legal frameworks in protecting victims of domestic abuse. It also spurred renewed focus on the psychological impact of online harassment and the spread of misinformation. The need for improved media literacy and responsible reporting standards was underscored by the case's highly publicized nature.

The case highlights the vital need for continued conversations about domestic violence, its warning signs, and the importance of providing comprehensive support for victims. It serves as a stark reminder of the pervasive nature of domestic violence and the importance of increased public awareness, education, and improved legal protection for victims. The public's demand for justice in Gabby's case resonated far beyond the immediate circumstances of her death, highlighting critical societal needs for improved law enforcement responsiveness, renewed attention to domestic violence awareness, and a more equitable approach to investigating missing persons cases, regardless of race or socioeconomic background. The long-term impacts of Gabby's story continue to shape discussions and policy changes, showcasing the lasting influence of a single tragedy in shaping national conversations and legislative action. The case serves as a powerful reminder of the crucial need for continuous vigilance and improvement across various systems designed to protect vulnerable individuals.

Chapter Fifteen

The Aftermath Lessons Learned and Future Implications

The aftermath of Gabby Petito's tragic death reverberated far beyond the immediate shock and grief. It sparked a critical examination of various systems—law enforcement response, media coverage, and the very nature of online communication—and their roles in addressing domestic violence and missing person cases. The intense public scrutiny, while sometimes fueled by misinformation and speculation, ultimately led to important conversations and potential policy changes that could save lives in the future.

One of the most significant lessons learned from Gabby's case is the critical importance of early intervention in domestic violence situations. While the full extent of the abuse suffered by Gabby may not have been immediately apparent to law enforcement, the available evidence, including witness accounts and body camera footage from earlier interactions, suggests that warning signs were present. These signs, however, might have been missed or insufficiently acted upon due to various factors, including a lack of training, inadequate protocols, and possibly implicit biases. The case underscored the need for law enforcement agencies to receive comprehensive training on recognizing the subtle indicators of domestic abuse and to adopt more proactive approaches when dealing with such incidents. This means moving beyond a reactive approach, which often waits for a significant event to trigger intervention, to a more proactive approach that emphasizes early identification and prevention.

Beyond individual officer training, the case highlighted deficiencies in inter-agency communication and coordination. The initial response to Gabby's disappearance, hampered by jurisdictional issues and a lack of seamless information sharing between agencies, significantly impacted the efficiency of the investigation. The delay in escalating the case to a high-priority investigation, given the potential for foul play, serves as a cautionary tale. Improved protocols for information sharing and collaborative investigations between local, state, and federal agencies are crucial to prevent similar delays in future cases. Investing in better communication systems and training programs focused on inter-agency collaboration is essential to address this systemic flaw. Clearer guidelines on escalating cases involving potential domestic violence would also streamline the process and ensure faster responses.

The media's role in the Gabby Petito case was complex and multifaceted. While the intense media coverage helped to raise public awareness and exert pressure on law enforcement, it also contributed to the spread of misinformation and speculation. The constant flow of updates, often sourced from unofficial channels, created a confusing narrative that hindered the official investigation. This highlights the crucial need for responsible media coverage, emphasizing accuracy and avoiding premature conclusions. Journalists need to be mindful of the potential impact of their reporting, particularly in cases involving ongoing investigations. Increased media literacy education for the general public would also help citizens to critically evaluate information and avoid the spread of misinformation. A clear distinction between confirmed facts and speculation is critical in responsible reporting.

Social media played a significant and controversial role. On one hand, social media's rapid dissemination of information aided in the swift mobilization of public support and assisted in accelerating the search for Gabby. Digital sleuths, using publicly available information, helped piece together timelines and identify potential evidence that might have otherwise gone unnoticed. However, the unfiltered and often unchecked nature of social media also contributed to the spread of misinformation, speculation, and even harassment of individuals involved in the case. The case showed a crucial need for responsible online behavior and the need for platforms to improve their mechanisms for identifying and removing harmful or misleading content. This requires a delicate balance: empowering citizens to use online platforms to contribute to investigations while mitigating the risks of misinformation and harmful online activity. The development of clearer guidelines and mechanisms for reporting misinformation and harassment on social media is essential for future cases.

The Gabby Petito case prompted a significant shift in the national conversation surrounding domestic violence. The public outpouring of grief and anger, fueled by the tragic circumstances, provided a powerful platform to discuss the prevalence and insidious nature of domestic abuse. The case served as a stark reminder of the need for continued awareness campaigns, improved support systems for victims, and increased funding for domestic violence prevention programs. Addressing domestic violence effectively requires a multifaceted approach. This includes strengthening legal protections for victims, improving access to shelters and support services, and challenging societal norms that contribute to the normalization of abusive behavior. Education programs focusing on the early warning signs of abusive relationships are also critical in preventing future tragedies.

The lasting implications of the Gabby Petito case extend far beyond individual tragedies. The heightened public awareness generated by the case has led to ongoing conversations regarding law enforcement protocols, media responsibility, and the role of social media in criminal investigations. Several jurisdictions have already begun to review and update their policies and training programs related to missing persons and domestic violence cases. This demonstrates a positive outcome in the wake of a tragedy, highlighting the power of public pressure in driving positive change.

Moving forward, the lessons learned from Gabby Petito's case must inform future investigative practices and policy decisions. This includes focusing on early intervention in domestic violence situations, improving inter-agency communication, ensuring responsible media coverage, and promoting responsible social media usage in criminal investigations. These are not isolated improvements; they are interconnected changes necessary for a more effective, compassionate, and just approach to handling missing persons cases and addressing the pervasive issue of domestic violence. Only through a comprehensive and sustained effort can we prevent similar tragedies and honor Gabby's memory by making real progress towards a safer future for everyone. The enduring impact of her story will continue to shape dialogues, inform policies, and, hopefully, lead to substantive changes in how we approach domestic violence and missing person investigations. The ultimate goal should be to ensure that the lessons from this heartbreaking case are not lost, but rather serve as a catalyst for positive and lasting systemic change.

Chapter Sixteen

Understanding the Dynamics of Abuse A Cycle of Violence

Understanding the cyclical nature of abuse is crucial to recognizing its insidious presence. It's not a linear progression of escalating violence; rather, it's a pattern characterized by periods of intense abuse followed by periods of remorse, affection, and even normalcy. This cycle, often referred to as the cycle of violence, can trap victims in a web of emotional and psychological manipulation, making it incredibly difficult to leave the relationship.

The initial phase, often romanticized as the "honeymoon phase," is marked by intense charm, affection, and idealization. The abuser showers the victim with attention, gifts, and promises, creating a seemingly perfect relationship. This period reinforces the victim's hope for a lasting and loving connection, making it harder to recognize the warning signs that may subtly emerge even in this early stage. Small instances of controlling behavior – such as subtly criticizing the victim's clothing choices or friendships – are often dismissed as quirks or minor issues. The victim may rationalize this behavior, attributing it to stress, insecurity, or even their own flaws. This phase is deceptively peaceful, masking the underlying pattern of abuse that will follow.

The second phase is the tension-building phase. The abuser's behavior gradually changes. They become irritable, unpredictable, and increasingly critical. Minor arguments escalate quickly, often with the abuser making unreasonable demands and accusations. The victim often feels a growing sense of anxiety and dread, constantly walking on eggshells to avoid triggering the abuser's anger. This phase can last for days, weeks, or even months, with the tension slowly simmering until it inevitably erupts.

This eruption marks the third phase: the acute battering incident. This is the most visible and often the most physically violent phase, but it's important to note that physical violence is not the only form of abuse. Verbal abuse, emotional manipulation, intimidation, economic control, and isolation are all forms of domestic violence, and these can occur with or without physical violence. During this acute battering incident, the abuser may lash out physically, verbally, or both. The intensity and nature of the violence can vary greatly, ranging from slapping and shoving to severe beatings and even life-threatening attacks. After this incident, the abuser may express remorse and apologize, shifting the blame onto the victim, claiming their actions were provoked, or minimizing the severity of the abuse.

Following the acute battering phase, the cycle often returns to the honeymoon phase. The abuser apologizes profusely, showering the victim with gifts, promises, and displays of affection. They may express deep remorse, swear it will never happen again, and even seek therapy or counseling. This period of reconciliation is crucial because it reinforces the victim's hope for change and prevents them from seeking outside help. The victim may feel guilty for reporting the abuse, fearing that their partner will become more violent if they leave. This cycle can continue for years, with each cycle potentially becoming more intense and more dangerous.

The cyclical nature of abuse is a powerful tool of control. It keeps victims trapped in a state of uncertainty and fear, making it difficult for them to leave the relationship. The periods of normalcy and affection reinforce the bond and create a false sense of hope, while the periods of abuse serve as a constant reminder of the abuser's power and control. The abuser skillfully manipulates the victim's emotions, leading to a dependence on their approval and creating a climate of fear that stifles independent thought and action.

One common tactic employed by abusers is isolation. They may restrict the victim's access to friends, family, and support systems, making them more dependent on the abuser. This isolation can be both physical, such as restricting movement or access to a phone or car, and emotional, such as controlling communication or constantly belittling the victim's support network. The abuser may spread rumors or lies about the victim, driving a wedge between them and their support systems. This isolates the victim further, making it challenging for them to seek help or escape the abusive relationship.

Financial control is another insidious tactic. Abusers may control the victim's finances, limiting access to funds or making them financially dependent on the abuser. This creates a sense of powerlessness and makes it even harder for the victim to leave. The abuser might prevent the victim from working, sabotage their employment opportunities, or withhold funds necessary for basic needs, such as food or shelter. This financial dependence creates a powerful barrier to escape and often leads to prolonged entrapment in the abusive cycle.

Emotional manipulation is a cornerstone of abusive relationships. Abusers use various tactics to manipulate the victim's emotions, such as gaslighting – making the victim doubt their own sanity and perception of reality – or using guilt and shame to control their behavior. They may minimize the abuse or deny its severity, placing the blame squarely on the victim. They may also use threats or intimidation to maintain control. The constant barrage of emotional manipulation wears down the victim's self-esteem, making them more dependent on the abuser for validation and approval.

The insidious nature of domestic abuse is often masked by seemingly normal aspects of the relationship. In public, the abuser may be charming and attentive, creating a stark contrast to their private behavior. This deception further isolates the victim, making it difficult for others to recognize the abuse. Friends and family may struggle to understand the situation, often dismissing concerns as relationship problems or suggesting the victim should "just leave". This lack of understanding and support only intensifies the victim's isolation and reinforces their feeling of helplessness.

Consider the case of Sarah and Mark. To the outside world, they seemed like a happy couple. Mark was successful, charming, and outgoing. Sarah, however, lived in constant fear. While Mark was publicly affectionate, he was privately controlling and verbally abusive. He monitored her calls, dictated her clothing choices, and constantly criticized her friends and family. Over time, Sarah became isolated and increasingly dependent on Mark for validation. The cycles of abuse, punctuated by periods of seemingly normal behavior and remorse, left her trapped, unable to see a way out, afraid to seek help and convinced it was her fault.

Another example is the case of Emily and David. Their relationship began idyllically, filled with romance and promises of a future together. As time passed, however, David's controlling behavior intensified. He monitored Emily's online activity, demanded constant updates on her location, and became increasingly jealous of her male colleagues. He frequently used insults and intimidation to control her, and although there was no physical violence, the constant emotional pressure and intimidation created a climate of fear and desperation. Emily found herself increasingly isolated and unable to confide in friends or family, who she feared wouldn't understand the subtle but pervasive emotional control that was slowly destroying her self-esteem.

These are just two examples among countless others. The common thread is the cyclical nature of the abuse, the subtle tactics employed by the abusers, and the isolating effect on the victim. Recognizing these patterns is crucial in identifying and addressing domestic violence. It requires understanding that abuse is not always overt and dramatic, but can manifest in many subtle and insidious ways. Early intervention and support are essential to break the cycle and help victims find a path to safety and independence. Ultimately, recognizing the dynamics of abuse is paramount in challenging societal norms that allow such violence to persist, fostering support systems that empower victims, and cultivating safer communities for everyone. The stories of Sarah and Emily highlight the need for increased awareness and understanding of the subtle signs of abuse to prevent similar tragedies from occurring. Education and early intervention are critical in combating this devastating problem.

Chapter Seventeen

Identifying Red Flags Verbal Emotional and Physical Abuse

Identifying the insidious nature of domestic abuse requires a keen awareness of its multifaceted presentation. While physical violence often grabs the headlines, it's crucial to understand that abuse manifests in various forms, each capable of inflicting deep psychological wounds and creating a climate of fear and control. Verbal abuse, emotional manipulation, and even seemingly innocuous controlling behaviors are all significant red flags demanding immediate attention. Recognizing these subtle signs is often the first step towards breaking free from the cycle of violence.

Verbal abuse is a pervasive and often underestimated form of domestic violence. It goes beyond the occasional harsh word or disagreement; it involves a pattern of belittling, insulting, humiliating, and threatening remarks aimed at degrading the victim's self-worth. This might include constant criticism, name-calling, insults targeting physical appearance or intelligence, and threats of violence or harm. The abuser might use sarcasm, mockery, and belittling tones to undermine the victim's confidence and control their behavior. The cumulative effect of this constant barrage of negativity can be devastating, eroding the victim's self-esteem and leaving them feeling worthless and helpless.

Consider the case of Anna and David, a couple who appeared outwardly successful and happy. David, however, routinely subjected Anna to verbal attacks, often in front of their friends and family. He would make snide comments about her cooking, her career choices, and even her parenting skills. Initially, Anna dismissed these remarks as mere jokes or expressions of frustration. However, the consistent negativity chipped away at her confidence, leaving her feeling increasingly inadequate and ashamed. David's comments, although not physically violent, created a constant atmosphere of anxiety and fear, making it difficult for her to express her thoughts and opinions without facing ridicule and criticism. This pattern of verbal abuse gradually escalated, eventually isolating Anna from her support network and leaving her feeling trapped.

Emotional abuse is another subtle yet destructive form of domestic violence. It involves a systematic effort to manipulate, control, and undermine the victim's emotional well-being. This can manifest in various ways, including gaslighting, where the abuser manipulates the victim into questioning their own sanity and perception of reality. They might deny events that occurred, twist facts, and make the victim doubt their memories and experiences, leaving them confused and disoriented. Emotional abusers often use guilt, shame, and manipulation to control their partner's behavior. They might use threats of abandonment, suicide, or self- harm to keep the victim in line, exploiting their partner's empathy and compassion to maintain control.

Take, for example, the situation faced by Maria and John. While there was no physical violence, John controlled Maria's every move through emotional manipulation. He'd make her feel guilty for spending time with friends, calling her selfish and inconsiderate. He'd twist her words and actions, making her believe she was always in the wrong, even when she knew she wasn't. This constant barrage of guilt and manipulation eroded Maria's self-confidence, making her increasingly dependent on John for validation and approval. She became isolated from her friends and family, convinced she was the problem and that John was the only one who could understand her. This emotional abuse created a profound sense of isolation and self-doubt, leaving her trapped in a relationship that was slowly destroying her sense of self.

Physical abuse, the most visible form of domestic violence, involves any form of physical harm or violence inflicted on a partner. This ranges from slapping and pushing to more serious acts such as punching, kicking, strangulation, and the use of weapons. The severity of physical violence can escalate over time, starting with minor incidents and progressing to more severe and life-threatening attacks. The physical injuries are often accompanied by emotional trauma, leaving the victim with lasting psychological scars. However, it's crucial to recognize that physical abuse isn't always overtly violent; it can also include controlling behaviors such as restricting movement or access to resources.

The case of Lisa and Robert serves as a stark illustration. Initially, their arguments resulted in Robert pushing Lisa or grabbing her arm. Lisa minimized these incidents, believing that they were isolated occurrences stemming from stress or alcohol. However, over time, the physical violence escalated. What started as pushing and shoving turned into punches and kicks, leaving Lisa with bruises and injuries. Robert would then apologize profusely, blaming Lisa for provoking him, showering her with gifts and affection, only to repeat the cycle of violence. The physical abuse inflicted lasting emotional damage, leaving Lisa fearful and trapped.

Beyond the obvious forms of abuse, various controlling behaviors serve as critical red flags. These behaviors are designed to isolate the victim, limit their autonomy, and maintain a power imbalance. Controlling behavior can manifest in several ways, including monitoring online activity, restricting access to financial resources, controlling communication with family and friends, dictating clothing choices, monitoring location, and imposing unreasonable restrictions on daily activities. These behaviors may seem subtle at first, easily dismissed as concerns or expressions of love. However, they are designed to chip away at the victim's independence and self-esteem, making them increasingly dependent on the abuser.

Financial control is a significant component of abusive relationships. The abuser might restrict the victim's access to money, control bank accounts, prevent them from working, or withhold financial resources necessary for their basic needs. This financial dependence renders the victim vulnerable and unable to leave the relationship, exacerbating their feeling of helplessness and entrapment.

Isolation is another insidious tactic used by abusers. This involves systematically isolating the victim from their support network, limiting contact with friends, family, and colleagues. The abuser might spread rumors, discredit the victim's claims of abuse, or create conflict between the victim and their support system. This isolation leaves the victim feeling alone, helpless, and unable to seek help.

Recognizing these red flags is crucial. It's important to remember that abuse is not always a dramatic event; it often begins subtly and escalates gradually. If you or someone you know is experiencing any of these signs, it's vital to seek help. There are resources available to provide support, guidance, and a path to safety. Remember, you are not alone, and help is available. Breaking the cycle of violence requires recognizing the warning signs, seeking support, and taking steps to ensure safety and well-being. The journey to recovery can be challenging, but it is possible to build a life free from abuse. Reaching out to a domestic violence hotline, a therapist, or a trusted friend or family member is a critical first step in reclaiming your life and breaking free from the cycle of abuse.

Chapter Eighteen

The Impact of Isolation and Control Tactics of Abuse

The insidious nature of domestic abuse often extends far beyond physical violence. A crucial element in understanding the dynamics of abusive relationships lies in recognizing the tactics abusers employ to isolate their victims and exert complete control. This control isn't simply about physical restraint; it's a meticulously crafted system of manipulation designed to erode the victim's self-esteem, independence, and connection to the outside world. Financial control, emotional manipulation, and gaslighting are potent tools in this arsenal, creating a web of dependence that makes escaping the relationship incredibly difficult.

Financial control is a pervasive tactic used to subjugate victims and maintain power imbalances. Abusers may deliberately restrict access to funds, controlling bank accounts, credit cards, and other financial resources. They might prevent their partners from working, sabotaging job opportunities or undermining their career aspirations. This deliberate economic dependence is a powerful tool for control, leaving victims feeling trapped and unable to leave, even if they desperately want to. They are rendered financially vulnerable, dependent on their abuser for even basic necessities like food, shelter, and transportation. The abuser's control over finances extends beyond mere material resources; it also controls access to independence and agency. This economic subjugation erodes the victim's self- worth and sense of self-sufficiency, further solidifying the abuser's dominance in the relationship.

Consider the situation faced by Sarah, whose abuser controlled all aspects of their shared finances. He monitored every penny spent, questioning every purchase, and routinely withholding money for necessities. Sarah, initially unaware of the manipulative nature of this control, eventually found herself completely dependent on him for even small amounts of cash. Attempts to seek employment were met with threats and intimidation, effectively trapping her in a cycle of financial dependence and abuse. This financial control amplified her feelings of isolation and helplessness, making escape seem impossible. Her social life diminished as the lack of funds prevented her from engaging in activities that might have fostered a support network outside of the abusive relationship. The control exerted over her finances mirrored the control exerted over other aspects of her life, creating an atmosphere of fear and desperation.

Beyond financial control, emotional manipulation is another cornerstone of abusive relationships. This tactic involves a calculated and systematic effort to undermine the victim's self-worth and emotional stability. Constant criticism, belittling remarks, and subtle forms of intimidation are all tools used to erode the victim's confidence and create a dependence on the abuser for validation. Gaslighting, a particularly insidious form of emotional manipulation, involves twisting reality and making the victim question their own sanity. The abuser might deny events that occurred, distort facts, and make the victim doubt their own memories and perceptions.

In the case of Emily, her partner consistently used gaslighting as a tool for control. He would deny arguments, distort conversations, and suggest that Emily was overly emotional or imagining things. Over time, this constant barrage of manipulation created a profound sense of self-doubt and confusion. Emily began to question her own memories and perceptions, believing her partner's version of events even when her own instincts told her otherwise. This erosion of self-trust made her increasingly reliant on her partner for validation, further entrenching her in the abusive relationship. Her attempts to discuss these issues were often met with anger, further isolating her and reinforcing her feeling that she was the problem.

The isolation of victims from their support systems is a crucial element in abusive relationships. This isolation is not merely accidental; it is a deliberate tactic designed to cut the victim off from friends, family, and other sources of support. Abusers might employ various strategies to achieve this, such as restricting access to phones or computers, monitoring online activity, and spreading rumors or lies about the victim to damage their reputation. They might also try to create conflict between the victim and their loved ones, driving wedges between the victim and their social network. This intentional isolation leaves the victim feeling vulnerable, alone, and dependent on the abuser for emotional support, creating an atmosphere of fear and control.

The case of Jessica illustrates this isolating behavior acutely. Her abuser gradually restricted her contact with her family and friends. He would subtly criticize her relationships with them, suggesting that they were jealous or did not understand their relationship. He monitored her phone calls and texts, limiting her communication. Eventually, Jessica found herself completely isolated, with no one outside the relationship to turn to for support or advice. This isolation served to reinforce her dependence on the abuser, leaving her feeling trapped and helpless. The fear of further conflict and the erosion of her self-confidence prevented her from seeking outside assistance.

These tactics – financial control, emotional manipulation, and isolation – are frequently intertwined, creating a powerful system of control that makes it extremely difficult for victims to leave abusive relationships. The cumulative effect of these manipulative strategies can be devastating, leaving victims with deep psychological wounds and a profound sense of helplessness. Understanding these dynamics is crucial to recognizing and addressing the issue of domestic violence. Recognizing these manipulative tactics, even in seemingly subtle forms, is the first step toward intervention and support for those trapped in abusive relationships. It is also a crucial element in understanding the dynamics of high-profile cases, such as that of Gabby Petito, where the manipulative control exerted by the abuser contributed significantly to the tragic outcome. While the specifics of each case are unique, the underlying patterns of control and manipulation often bear striking similarities. The unraveling of these patterns, through investigation and careful analysis, is often key to understanding the dynamics of the abuse and the subsequent tragic events.

Chapter Nineteen

Breaking the Cycle Support Systems and Resources

Breaking free from the grip of domestic violence is a daunting, yet achievable, goal. The path to safety and recovery is often paved with challenges, but numerous resources and support systems exist to guide victims through this difficult journey. Understanding these resources and accessing them is crucial for escaping abusive situations and rebuilding a life free from fear and control. This section provides practical strategies and information for those seeking help, empowering them to take the first steps towards a safer future.

The initial step towards safety often involves recognizing that you are not alone. Domestic violence is a pervasive problem, and help is readily available. Many victims grapple with feelings of shame, guilt, or fear, believing they are somehow responsible for the abuse. It's imperative to understand that this is a false narrative perpetuated by the abuser. Abuse is never the victim's fault. The abuser's behavior is a reflection of their own issues, not a consequence of the victim's actions or character.

One crucial step involves creating a safety plan. This plan should be personalized and address the specific circumstances of your situation. It should include strategies for immediate safety, such as identifying safe places to go in case of an emergency, having a pre-packed bag ready to leave at a moment's notice, and memorizing emergency phone numbers. This plan should also consider longer-term strategies, including securing housing, financial independence, and legal assistance.

Financial independence is often a significant hurdle for victims of domestic violence. Abusers frequently control the finances, limiting the victim's access to funds and resources. Developing a plan to regain financial autonomy is crucial. This may involve seeking legal assistance to gain access to joint accounts, applying for public assistance programs, or finding employment. Several organizations offer financial assistance and job training specifically for victims of domestic violence. These resources can provide crucial support during the transition to financial independence, empowering victims to rebuild their lives without the financial constraints imposed by the abuser.

Legal aid is an essential component of escaping domestic violence. Obtaining a protective order can provide crucial legal protection and establish boundaries to prevent further abuse. Legal aid organizations offer free or low-cost legal services to victims, helping them navigate the legal system and secure the necessary protection. These services can include assistance with filing for divorce, custody arrangements, and restraining orders. They can also provide legal representation during court proceedings, advocating for the victim's safety and well-being. Understanding your legal rights and options is a crucial step in protecting yourself and securing a safe future.

Shelters provide a safe haven for victims of domestic violence, offering temporary housing and support services. These shelters provide a refuge from the abusive environment, offering a place to recover and regroup. They often provide counseling, legal aid, and assistance with job placement, helping victims rebuild their lives. Shelters vary in their services, but most offer a safe, confidential environment with access to crucial support services. Finding a local shelter can often be done through a simple online search, or by contacting a national domestic violence hotline.

Counseling services are critical for the healing process after escaping domestic violence. Many victims experience emotional trauma, including post-traumatic stress disorder (PTSD), anxiety, and depression. Professional counseling can provide a safe space to process these experiences, develop coping mechanisms, and rebuild self-esteem. Therapists specializing in trauma-informed care are particularly well-equipped to work with victims of domestic violence, ensuring a supportive and understanding environment. Many organizations offer free or low-cost counseling services, recognizing the importance of accessible mental health support for victims.

Support groups provide a valuable network of support for victims of domestic violence. Connecting with other survivors allows individuals to share experiences, receive encouragement, and feel less isolated in their struggles. These groups offer a sense of community and shared understanding, fostering a supportive environment where victims can learn from one another and gain strength from shared experiences. Many support groups operate both online and in person, providing options for victims to connect with others in a way that feels safe and comfortable.

Education and awareness are crucial in breaking the cycle of domestic violence. Raising public awareness about the signs of abuse, the dynamics of abusive relationships, and the availability of resources can help prevent future instances of violence and empower individuals to intervene when they see warning signs. By promoting education and awareness, we create a society that is better equipped to support victims and hold abusers accountable. This includes educating children and young people about healthy relationships and consent.

Technology has also played a significant role in both perpetrating and escaping domestic violence. Abusers often use technology to monitor and control their victims, using spyware, tracking apps, or social media surveillance. However, technology can also be a tool for escape and empowerment. There are apps and resources designed to help victims discreetly document abuse, access support networks, and find safety. Understanding these technologies is crucial for both prevention and escape.

The journey to safety and recovery from domestic violence is a complex and deeply personal one. There is no one-size- fits-all solution. However, a vast network of resources and support systems exists to help victims navigate this challenging period. By utilizing these resources, victims can take control of their lives, break free from abusive relationships, and begin the process of healing and rebuilding. Remembering that you are not alone and that help is available is the first crucial step on this journey.

Seeking support and utilizing available resources can pave the way to a safer, more fulfilling future, free from the constraints of abuse. The path may be challenging, but it is a path worth traveling, leading to a life of freedom, empowerment, and healing. The journey toward healing and rebuilding is long and demanding, but with perseverance and the support of available resources, a life free from fear and abuse is attainable. Remember, reaching out is a sign of strength, not weakness.

Chapter Twenty

Prevention and Intervention A Community Responsibility

Prevention and intervention in domestic violence extend far beyond the individual victim and abuser; they represent a critical responsibility shared by the entire community. A proactive approach, encompassing education, awareness, and readily accessible support systems, is crucial in disrupting the cycle of abuse and fostering safer environments for everyone. This requires a collective commitment from individuals, organizations, and local authorities to create a culture where violence is unacceptable and help is readily available.

One of the most effective strategies for preventing domestic violence is comprehensive education. This begins early, integrating age-appropriate lessons on healthy relationships, consent, and respect into school curricula from elementary school onwards. Such education should move beyond simple definitions of abuse, exploring power dynamics, manipulation tactics, and the subtle signs of unhealthy relationships. It should empower young people to recognize red flags, understand their rights, and develop healthy communication and conflict-resolution skills. Furthermore, incorporating bystander intervention training into these programs is essential, equipping young people with the tools to safely and effectively intervene when they witness abusive behavior among their peers. These programs shouldn't just be theoretical exercises; they should offer practical scenarios and role-playing to solidify learning and build confidence in intervention.

Adult education initiatives are equally crucial. Community workshops, public awareness campaigns, and online resources can inform adults about the prevalence of domestic violence, its devastating impact, and the available resources for victims and those seeking to help. These campaigns should highlight the different forms domestic violence can take, including physical, emotional, verbal, financial, and sexual abuse. Often, abuse is masked under the guise of a "loving relationship" making it critical to educate the public about subtle signs of control and manipulation, including isolating tactics, constant criticism, possessiveness, and threats. Using real-life case studies (while protecting victim identities, of course) can be powerful tools in conveying the gravity and nuances of this issue. These case studies, if used appropriately, can show how seemingly small instances of controlling behavior can escalate into serious violence.

Community-based programs play a vital role in prevention and intervention. These programs might include support groups for victims and their families, educational workshops for at-risk individuals and their partners, and counseling services for abusers who are willing to participate in rehabilitation programs. Successful programs frequently involve a multidisciplinary approach, bringing together law enforcement, social workers, mental health professionals, and community advocates to provide holistic support. Early intervention programs, focusing on families exhibiting high- risk factors such as intergenerational trauma or substance abuse, are particularly valuable in preventing the transmission of violent behavior across generations. The effectiveness of these programs is significantly enhanced by collaboration with existing community organizations, such as churches, schools, and community centers, to maximize reach and accessibility.

However, prevention efforts are only truly effective when coupled with robust intervention strategies. This means creating a system where victims feel safe to report abuse without fear of judgment or retaliation. This requires improved training for law enforcement, social workers, and healthcare professionals to appropriately respond to reports of domestic violence, ensuring victims' safety and dignity are prioritized. It means implementing effective and consistent policies regarding protective orders, ensuring they are readily accessible and rigorously enforced. It also means providing accessible and comprehensive support services for victims, including emergency shelter, legal aid, counseling, and financial assistance.

The role of bystanders in preventing and intervening in domestic violence cannot be overstated. Often, friends, family members, and neighbors witness abusive behaviors without knowing how to respond. Educating the public about safe and effective ways to intervene is crucial. Bystanders should not feel obligated to confront an abuser directly, particularly if it puts themselves at risk. Instead, they can take steps such as contacting the authorities, offering support to the victim, or documenting instances of abuse. Training programs emphasizing de-escalation techniques, safety precautions, and the importance of reporting can equip bystanders with the necessary skills to intervene safely and effectively. These programs should also stress the importance of believing victims and providing unconditional support, avoiding any behaviors that might inadvertently blame or shame the victim.

Creating safer communities requires a multi-faceted approach that addresses the root causes of domestic violence. This includes addressing issues such as poverty, inequality, and lack of access to resources, all of which can increase the risk of abuse. Community-based initiatives focused on promoting economic empowerment, providing access to affordable housing and childcare, and addressing substance abuse can help create environments where families are more resilient and less prone to violence. Furthermore, public health campaigns should aim to challenge harmful gender stereotypes and norms that contribute to the acceptance of violence against women and children. These campaigns should be inclusive and address different cultural contexts, promoting healthy relationships and respect for individual autonomy.

In conclusion, the prevention and intervention of domestic violence is not solely the responsibility of law enforcement or social services; it is a shared responsibility of the entire community. A comprehensive strategy, incorporating education, awareness, accessible resources, and community-based programs, is vital in disrupting the cycle of violence and building safer communities for everyone. By fostering a culture of respect, accountability, and support, we can create environments where victims feel empowered to seek help and where abusers are held accountable for their actions. This requires ongoing commitment, collaboration, and a collective determination to address this pervasive issue, ensuring that every individual has the right to live free from fear and violence. The long-term success hinges on a sustained commitment to education, intervention, and community-wide support—a collective pledge to create a society where domestic violence is not merely addressed but ultimately eradicated.

Chapter Twenty-One

Remembering Gabby Beyond the Headlines

Gabby Petito's story transcended the realm of a typical missing person's case; it became a national obsession, a chilling spectacle played out on screens across the country. But behind the grainy police bodycam footage, the viral social media posts, and the relentless news cycle, was a young woman with a life, dreams, and a personality that deserved to be remembered beyond the tragic circumstances of her death. This section aims to peel back the layers of media sensationalism and reveal the vibrant, ambitious, and deeply loved Gabby Petito.

Her family and friends describe her as an adventurous soul, a free spirit with an infectious laugh and a kind heart. She wasn't just a pretty face in a van life Instagram post; she was a dedicated aspiring travel blogger, meticulously documenting her journey across the country, sharing her experiences with a growing online audience. Those who knew her intimately describe her passion for photography, her love for capturing the beauty of the natural world, and her innate ability to connect with people from all walks of life. This wasn't simply a curated online persona; her social media presence genuinely reflected her adventurous and enthusiastic personality. Photos from her childhood, unearthed by the media and shared by her family, painted a picture of a happy, playful child, brimming with curiosity and a zest for life. These aren't just static images; they offer a glimpse into the development of a young woman who was clearly passionate about experiences and building memories.

Beyond her online presence, countless anecdotes from her family and friends paint a much fuller picture of Gabby. Stories of her childhood adventures, her close relationships with her siblings, and her strong bond with her parents reveal a young woman who was deeply loved and cherished. Her mother, Nichole Schmidt, often spoke of Gabby's unwavering optimism, her determination to overcome challenges, and her infectious enthusiasm for life. These aren't just emotional tributes; they are tangible memories that provide a counterpoint to the often-distorted media narrative that focused solely on the tragic end of her story. These personal reflections offer a poignant glimpse into a young woman filled with hope and dreams, a young woman who embraced life with open arms, leaving behind a legacy of kindness and adventure.

The impact of her story on her immediate family, particularly her parents, has been profound and lasting. The loss of Gabby is a wound that will never fully heal. Yet, in the midst of their unspeakable grief, they have channeled their pain into a force for positive change, dedicating themselves to advocating for victims of domestic violence and working tirelessly to prevent similar tragedies from occurring. This is a testament to Gabby's spirit and the enduring strength of her family. Their efforts serve as a powerful reminder of the ripple effect of domestic violence and the importance of advocating for justice and reform. Their advocacy is not merely a response to their grief; it is a dedication to ensuring that other families never experience the unimaginable pain they have endured.

Numerous interviews with friends and colleagues reveal a consistently positive narrative. Gabby's personality wasn't confined to the curated world of social media; she maintained authentic relationships, demonstrating kindness, empathy, and unwavering support for those around her. These accounts highlight her warmth, her generosity, and her deep capacity for love and friendship. The recollections are far more nuanced and enriching than the brief, often sensationalized portrayals that emerged during the initial media frenzy. These firsthand accounts provide a crucial corrective to the often-incomplete and misleading narratives that dominated the early coverage of her case. They humanize Gabby, reminding us that she was more than just a victim; she was a beloved daughter, sister, and friend.

Beyond the personal accounts, Gabby's aspirations further reveal her character. Her passion for travel and adventure was not a fleeting fancy; it was deeply rooted in a desire to experience the world and share her experiences with others. Her dedication to her travel blog reflects a drive to create, to share, and to connect with a wider community. This ambition wasn't just about achieving online fame; it was about documenting her experiences, sharing her love of nature, and inspiring others to explore and appreciate the world around them. Her meticulously documented journey, a mix of stunning photos and heartfelt reflections, speaks volumes about her commitment, her personality, and her aspirations. These weren't fleeting snapshots; they represent a thoughtful and planned approach to documenting her adventures.

The tragic circumstances surrounding Gabby's death have understandably overshadowed her life and aspirations. However, remembering Gabby is not just about acknowledging her tragic end; it is about celebrating the life she lived, the person she was, and the impact she had on those around her. Her story should not be defined solely by violence; it should be remembered as a testament to a vibrant young woman with dreams, ambition, and a zest for life. By remembering her in this way, we honor her memory and prevent her story from becoming another statistic in the grim reality of domestic violence. We remember her not just as a victim but as a force of nature, a young woman with big dreams and a bigger heart, cut short far too soon.

Her legacy extends beyond her immediate circle. Her story sparked a national conversation about domestic violence, prompting greater awareness and a renewed focus on prevention and intervention. The intense media scrutiny and public outcry that followed her disappearance highlighted the urgent need for improved support systems for victims, stricter enforcement of laws related to domestic abuse, and increased education to help identify and address the early warning signs of abusive relationships. While the tragic circumstances surrounding her death are undeniable, her story has inadvertently led to positive changes, creating a more informed and responsive approach to tackling domestic violence. This is a testament to her influence, extending far beyond the headlines and the court proceedings.

In conclusion, remembering Gabby Petito necessitates a conscious shift from the often sensationalized media narrative to a more human, nuanced understanding of her life and personality. It's a call to acknowledge the vibrancy of her spirit, her adventurous nature, and her aspirations. By focusing on the personal accounts of her loved ones, by highlighting her passions and dreams, and by understanding the impact her story has had on societal awareness of domestic violence, we can truly honor her legacy. Her story is not merely a tragic tale; it's a call for change, a potent reminder of the importance of recognizing the signs of abuse, protecting victims, and fostering a culture of respect and support for those who need it most. Gabby's life, although tragically cut short, continues to inspire action, compassion, and a renewed commitment to creating a safer world for all. The lasting impact of her story will be measured not just in headlines, but in the changes it has brought and will continue to bring about in our fight against domestic violence and promoting safer communities. Her memory demands that we not simply remember her, but that we work to prevent future tragedies by learning from her story.

Chapter Twenty-Two

The Impact on Domestic Violence Awareness

The tragic death of Gabby Petito undeniably cast a harsh spotlight on the pervasive issue of domestic violence. While the circumstances surrounding her disappearance and death were horrific, the intense media coverage and public outcry that followed had an undeniable and largely positive impact on domestic violence awareness, sparking crucial conversations and prompting significant changes in how the issue is perceived and addressed. Prior to Gabby's case becoming a national news story, discussions surrounding domestic violence, while present, often lacked the widespread urgency and public understanding that followed. Her story, tragically, served as a catalyst, forcing a nation to confront a problem that had been largely relegated to the shadows.

The sheer volume of media attention dedicated to Gabby's case created an unprecedented level of public awareness about domestic violence. News outlets, social media platforms, and even online forums were saturated with discussions about the case, its potential connection to domestic abuse, and the broader implications for relationship dynamics and societal responses to violence. This intense scrutiny forced many to confront their own preconceived notions about domestic violence, challenging stereotypes and myths that often hinder both identification and intervention. The readily available images and videos – initially shared on social media by Gabby and Brian, later used in news reports – highlighted the subtle yet insidious nature of abusive behavior. These visual aids went far beyond mere statistics and provided a tangible representation of the emotional and psychological toll of domestic violence on victims.

Before Gabby's case, public awareness campaigns focused on domestic violence often suffered from limited reach and impact. While organizations like the National Coalition Against Domestic Violence (NCADV) had been working tirelessly to raise awareness, their message often struggled to penetrate the public consciousness. Gabby's story, however, transcended the limitations of traditional awareness campaigns, reaching a vast and diverse audience through a variety of media channels. This widespread reach allowed for a much broader understanding of the complexities of domestic violence, moving beyond simplistic narratives and acknowledging the nuances of abusive relationships.

Quantifying the impact of Gabby's case requires careful consideration. While precise causal links are difficult to establish, anecdotal evidence and statistical trends suggest a notable increase in reported domestic violence cases and related support-seeking behaviors following the intense media coverage. Analyzing data from national hotlines and domestic violence shelters, both before and after the period of heightened public attention, provides valuable insights.

While this data may not directly attribute a specific percentage increase solely to Gabby's case, it does highlight a significant upward trend in reported cases and calls for help during this period, suggesting a correlation between increased awareness and greater willingness to seek assistance. It's crucial to understand that this increase might also be influenced by other factors, but Gabby's case undoubtedly played a role in shifting public perception, encouraging more victims to come forward.

Moreover, the heightened attention sparked by Gabby's case led to renewed discussions and debates surrounding legal frameworks, enforcement mechanisms, and support systems for victims of domestic violence. Lawmakers, advocates, and legal professionals engaged in conversations about improving existing laws, enhancing protection orders, and strengthening resources for victims seeking refuge and support. The urgency of the situation, fueled by the intense public scrutiny, created an environment conducive to policy change and legislative action aimed at better supporting victims and holding perpetrators accountable. This focus on legal and systemic reforms highlighted a critical need to improve existing support systems, ensuring victims have access to necessary resources and protection.

The Gabby Petito case also stimulated vital conversations about the role of social media in both documenting and perpetuating violence. The initial sharing of Gabby and Brian's idyllic van life journey on social media provided a stark contrast to the dark reality that unfolded. This brought into focus the potential for social media to obscure or mask the signs of abusive relationships, highlighting the danger of relying solely on curated online personas to assess the health of a relationship. Simultaneously, it also underscored the power of social media in raising awareness, mobilizing public support, and facilitating the rapid dissemination of information, crucial aspects in high-profile missing person cases. This dual nature of social media – both a potential space for masking abuse and a powerful tool for raising awareness – necessitated a more critical understanding of how online platforms are used and the potential impact on discussions surrounding domestic violence.

Another significant impact of Gabby's case was a heightened focus on identifying and addressing the early warning signs of abusive relationships. Prior to the case, many individuals might have overlooked or minimized subtle signs of control, manipulation, and emotional abuse. The intense scrutiny of Gabby and Brian's relationship, however, allowed for a more thorough examination of these patterns, fostering a better understanding of the dynamics of abusive relationships. The analysis of Gabby's interactions with Brian, through their social media posts, videos, and witness accounts, helped identify common red flags that often precede escalating violence. This led to broader discussions about the importance of recognizing these subtle signs, not just in romantic relationships, but across all types of interpersonal interactions.

The aftermath of Gabby's death also highlighted the importance of interagency collaboration in addressing domestic violence. Law enforcement agencies, social service organizations, and mental health providers found themselves working more closely together, sharing information and coordinating responses to domestic violence incidents. This increased collaboration demonstrated the necessity of a multi-faceted approach to tackling the complex problem of domestic violence, requiring coordinated efforts across various sectors to effectively address its root causes and provide comprehensive support to survivors. The success of this collaborative response emphasized the need for ongoing and improved communication and resource-sharing between different agencies to better protect victims and prevent future tragedies.

In conclusion, while the death of Gabby Petito was a deeply tragic event, her story inadvertently spurred significant advancements in domestic violence awareness and prevention. The intense media coverage, coupled with the public outcry, led to a heightened understanding of the dynamics of abuse, improved identification of early warning signs, and increased willingness to seek help. Moreover, the case prompted crucial conversations about legal reforms, improved support systems, and the responsible use of social media. While statistical data may not perfectly capture the full extent of the impact, the anecdotal evidence, coupled with observable trends in reported cases and legislative actions, suggests a tangible and significant positive shift in addressing this complex and pervasive issue. The legacy of Gabby Petito, while born of tragedy, serves as a powerful catalyst for positive change, reminding us that even in the face of unimaginable loss, progress is possible, and the fight for a safer world continues.

Chapter Twenty-Three

Reforming Law Enforcement Response to Domestic Violence

The Gabby Petito case, while deeply tragic, served as a stark reminder of the shortcomings in law enforcement's response to domestic violence. The investigation, scrutinized intensely by the public and media, revealed critical gaps in how such cases are handled, highlighting the need for significant reforms across the nation. One of the most glaring issues exposed was the initial reluctance, in some instances, to fully investigate reported instances of domestic abuse. The "he said, she said" dynamic, often cited as a reason for inaction, proved to be a deeply flawed approach, particularly given the potential lethality of domestic violence. Gabby's case underscores the urgent need to move beyond this simplistic binary and adopt a more proactive, victim-centered approach.

Before Gabby's case gained national attention, many law enforcement agencies lacked standardized protocols for handling domestic violence calls. While mandatory arrest laws exist in some jurisdictions, their implementation and effectiveness varied significantly across different regions and departments. The lack of consistent training and standardized procedures led to inconsistent responses, with some officers prioritizing de-escalation over immediate intervention, potentially putting victims at greater risk. The investigation into Gabby's case highlighted the dangers of this approach. While the exact sequence of events remains a subject of debate, the failure to thoroughly investigate earlier reported incidents of alleged domestic disputes between Gabby and Brian Laundrie casts a critical shadow on the effectiveness of the initial law enforcement response.

A critical element often overlooked in domestic violence cases is the role of power and control dynamics. Abuse is rarely a single isolated incident; it's a pattern of behavior designed to exert control over the victim. Law enforcement officers require training to recognize the subtle yet insidious signs of manipulative behavior – financial control, emotional manipulation, isolation from friends and family, threats, intimidation, and coercive control. Gabby's case highlighted how such patterns can escalate to lethal violence if not properly addressed. Future training programs must emphasize the identification of these subtle cues, moving beyond a narrow focus on physical violence alone. The training should include real-life case studies, including analyses of cases similar to Gabby's, to illustrate how these subtle dynamics can evolve into deadly situations.

The investigation also brought to light the significant challenges in effectively collecting and preserving digital evidence. In today's digital age, social media posts, text messages, and other online interactions can provide critical insights into the dynamics of an abusive relationship. However, law enforcement agencies often lack the expertise and resources to properly gather, analyze, and utilize this crucial evidence. The delay in accessing and analyzing Brian Laundrie's phone and computer data underscores the need for improved training in digital forensics for law enforcement personnel involved in domestic violence investigations. A significant investment in technological infrastructure and specialized training is required to ensure that digital evidence is properly handled and utilized in these investigations. This includes not just the technical expertise but also the legal framework and ethical considerations in accessing such information, balancing privacy concerns with the need to ensure justice for victims.

Another area where reform is urgently needed is interagency collaboration. Domestic violence cases often require coordination between law enforcement, social services, mental health professionals, and victim advocacy groups.

The fragmented nature of these services can hinder effective intervention and support for victims. The Gabby Petito case demonstrated the limitations of a disjointed approach, where critical information might not be shared effectively between agencies, hindering the investigation and leaving victims vulnerable. This calls for better communication protocols, shared databases, and joint training initiatives to foster a more unified response to domestic violence. This coordinated approach should also include the implementation of risk assessment tools that can better predict the likelihood of future violence and allow for proactive intervention.

The role of victim support services and shelters is equally critical. Victims of domestic violence often require immediate access to safe housing, counseling, legal assistance, and other crucial resources. The availability and accessibility of these services vary widely across different jurisdictions. In some areas, limited resources and funding lead to long waitlists and insufficient support for victims. Gabby Petito's case highlighted the urgent need to expand and enhance the availability of these vital support systems, ensuring that victims have immediate access to the help they need, regardless of their location or financial circumstances. This requires significant investment in infrastructure, staffing, and community outreach programs to ensure that support services are readily available to all victims.

The training of law enforcement officers in handling domestic violence cases requires a fundamental shift in perspective. The focus needs to move away from a reactive approach, prioritizing immediate intervention and victim safety, to a more proactive and preventative strategy. This requires training that goes beyond the basics of responding to domestic violence calls. It needs to encompass a deep understanding of the dynamics of abuse, including the complexities of power and control, the identification of subtle signs of abuse, and the importance of victim-centered interviewing techniques. This holistic approach necessitates ongoing and updated training incorporating best practices from around the world and incorporating feedback from survivors to better reflect their lived experiences and needs. The training should also focus on de-escalation techniques, crisis intervention strategies, and the importance of listening to and believing victims.

The legal landscape surrounding domestic violence also requires careful examination. While mandatory arrest laws exist in many jurisdictions, their effectiveness varies, and some jurisdictions still lack such laws. The Gabby Petito case highlights the need for consistent and strong legal frameworks across all jurisdictions. Moreover, the legal system should offer more protection for victims, streamlining the process of obtaining protection orders, providing increased access to legal aid, and enhancing the enforcement of restraining orders. These legal improvements should be supported by extensive public education campaigns to raise awareness about the rights of victims and the available legal recourse.

Finally, the Gabby Petito case serves as a powerful reminder of the role of technology and social media in both perpetuating and exposing domestic violence. While social media can be used to mask the reality of abusive relationships, it can also be a valuable tool for documenting evidence and raising awareness. Law enforcement agencies need to be trained on how to effectively leverage social media and other digital platforms in their investigations, while also addressing the ethical concerns surrounding the privacy rights of individuals. This includes developing strategies to responsibly access and utilize digital evidence, while also considering the potential for online harassment and victim shaming.

In conclusion, reforming law enforcement's response to domestic violence requires a multi-pronged approach. It necessitates better training for officers, improved interagency collaboration, expanded access to victim support services, stronger legal frameworks, and a deeper understanding of the role of technology in these cases. The legacy of Gabby Petito should not be merely a tragedy, but a catalyst for significant and lasting change, ensuring that future victims receive the support and protection they desperately need. The lessons learned from her case should be used to create a system where domestic violence is not only investigated effectively but also prevented, ultimately creating a safer environment for all.

Chapter Twenty-Four

Improving Support for Victims of Domestic Violence

The tragic death of Gabby Petito exposed a critical gap in our societal response to domestic violence: the inadequate support systems available to victims. While law enforcement reform is crucial, equally important is the creation of a robust, accessible, and comprehensive network of support designed to empower victims to escape abusive situations and rebuild their lives. The current system, fragmented and often under-resourced, leaves many victims feeling isolated, vulnerable, and without the tools they need to break free.

One of the most immediate and vital needs for victims of domestic violence is safe housing. Shelters, often the first line of defense, frequently face overwhelming demand, leaving many victims without a place to escape immediate danger. The scarcity of shelter beds is a nationwide problem, exacerbated by insufficient funding and a lack of affordable housing options in general. Expansion of shelter capacity, coupled with the creation of transitional housing programs that provide longer-term support and assistance with finding permanent housing, is critical. Innovative solutions, such as partnering with hotels or motels to provide temporary housing during peak demand or utilizing existing community spaces, should be explored.

Beyond safe housing, victims require immediate access to legal assistance. Navigating the legal system during a time of trauma can be incredibly daunting. Many victims are unaware of their legal rights, unable to afford legal representation, or struggle to effectively communicate their experiences within the legal framework. Increased funding for legal aid programs specifically focused on domestic violence cases is imperative, ensuring that victims have access to skilled attorneys who can help them obtain protection orders, pursue criminal charges against their abusers, and secure custody arrangements for their children if applicable. Pro bono legal services and readily available legal information, translated into multiple languages to accommodate diverse communities, must also be prioritized.

Counseling and therapy play a vital role in the healing process. The psychological impact of domestic violence can be profound and long-lasting, often resulting in PTSD, depression, anxiety, and other mental health challenges. Access to trauma-informed therapists who understand the dynamics of abuse and are equipped to provide effective support is crucial. This requires expanding mental health services, specifically training therapists on working with victims of domestic violence and ensuring that such services are affordable and accessible to all victims regardless of their socioeconomic background. Telehealth platforms can broaden the reach of these critical services, particularly in rural or underserved areas where access to in-person care might be limited.

Financial independence is another cornerstone of escaping abusive relationships. Many victims are financially dependent on their abusers, leaving them with limited options for leaving. Job training programs, financial literacy workshops, and assistance with securing employment are critical components of support services. This could include collaborating with local businesses to create job opportunities specifically designed to support victims, or partnering with vocational schools to provide skills training that leads to stable employment. Micro-loans or financial assistance programs could also empower victims to achieve financial independence and build a new life free from abuse.

Children are often deeply affected by domestic violence, witnessing the abuse firsthand and experiencing its emotional and psychological consequences. Specialized services for children who have witnessed domestic violence are critical. This includes child-centered therapy, support groups for children of domestic abuse survivors, and educational programs designed to help children understand the dynamics of abuse and the importance of seeking help. Schools can play a pivotal role in identifying children affected by domestic violence and linking them with appropriate resources.

Community-based support programs offer an essential lifeline for victims. These programs can provide a network of support, connecting victims with peer advocates, support groups, and community resources. These groups offer a safe space for victims to share their experiences, build resilience, and develop coping mechanisms. Community awareness campaigns can help educate the public about the signs of domestic violence and encourage people to intervene safely when witnessing potential instances of abuse. These programs should also provide support for friends and family members of victims, equipping them with the tools to offer effective assistance and understand the complexities of domestic violence.

Technology plays a dual role in domestic violence. It can be used by abusers to control and monitor victims, but it also offers a powerful tool for victims to document abuse, seek help, and connect with support networks. This necessitates increased training for both victims and those who support them on how to safely and effectively use technology to document abuse and maintain online safety. Law enforcement agencies should also receive training on how to properly handle and analyze digital evidence in domestic violence cases.

The Gabby Petito case, though tragic, spurred a national conversation on domestic violence. This momentum should be harnessed to create lasting change in how we support victims. This requires not just increased funding for existing programs, but a fundamental shift in approach. It necessitates a victim-centered system, prioritizing their safety, well-being, and empowerment. This means investing in comprehensive support services, including safe housing, legal aid, counseling, financial assistance, child support services, and community-based programs. It means ensuring accessibility across all demographics, addressing the needs of diverse communities, and breaking down systemic barriers that prevent victims from accessing the help they need.

The path toward creating truly effective support systems for victims of domestic violence is a long one, demanding collaboration across various sectors, including law enforcement, social services, mental health providers, legal professionals, and community organizations. This requires a multi-pronged strategy: increased funding, innovative approaches, improved data collection and analysis, effective collaboration among organizations, and continued public awareness campaigns that destigmatize domestic violence. The legacy of Gabby Petito demands a comprehensive and sustained commitment to building a society that protects victims, empowers them to rebuild their lives, and ultimately prevents domestic violence from ever happening in the first place. Only through collective action and a concerted national effort can we hope to create a future where such tragedies are far less common.

Chapter Twenty-Five

The Enduring Legacy of Gabby A Call to Action

The outpouring of grief and support following Gabby Petito's death was unprecedented. Her story, amplified by social media and the relentless coverage of the news, became a rallying cry for change, forcing a national conversation about domestic violence that had previously been too often hushed. Yet, the intense media focus, while undeniably crucial in bringing the issue to light, also highlighted the complexities and inherent challenges in tackling this pervasive problem. The sheer volume of online commentary, from heartfelt condolences to armchair detective work, underscored both the public's thirst for justice and the potential pitfalls of relying solely on social media for solutions. The digital deluge surrounding Gabby's case, while useful in raising awareness, also demonstrated the need for careful discernment and a structured, professional approach to addressing domestic violence.

The speed and intensity of the public response, fueled by the readily available visual evidence, exposed a stark contrast to the often-lengthy and arduous processes victims face when seeking help. Gabby's case, with its seemingly straightforward narrative of a missing young woman and a seemingly uncooperative fiancé, contrasted sharply with the lived realities of many victims who face complex legal battles, systemic barriers, and a lack of readily available resources. The intense media scrutiny also created an uneven playing field, where those with a high media profile might attract more attention and resources than others facing similar circumstances, reinforcing existing inequalities within the system.

One of the most important lessons learned from Gabby's case is the critical need for improved communication and collaboration between law enforcement agencies, social service providers, and victim support organizations. The fragmented nature of these support systems often leaves victims navigating a maze of agencies, with little coordination or consistency in the level of support offered. The early stages of the investigation into Gabby's disappearance, while eventually yielding results, highlighted the challenges of information sharing and effective collaboration across jurisdictional boundaries. Standardizing reporting procedures, establishing clear protocols for data sharing, and improving inter-agency communication are crucial steps in ensuring that victims receive timely and effective assistance regardless of their location.

Beyond improved inter-agency collaboration, a more comprehensive and proactive approach to domestic violence prevention is paramount. While reactive measures are essential to support victims in crisis, a focus on prevention can disrupt the cycle of abuse before it even begins. This requires educational programs targeting young people, beginning in schools, to address healthy relationships, consent, and identifying the signs of abuse. Community- based initiatives focused on promoting healthy masculinity and challenging harmful societal norms that normalize or excuse abusive behavior are equally important. Such programs require sustained funding and a long-term commitment to building a culture of respect and accountability.

The digital landscape, while a powerful tool for raising awareness and disseminating information, also presents unique challenges. Online harassment and cyberbullying, often extensions of domestic abuse, need to be addressed more effectively. The ease with which abusers can monitor and control their victims through technology necessitates enhanced digital literacy programs for victims, providing them with the tools and knowledge to protect themselves online. Training law enforcement on the use and retrieval of digital evidence is equally vital in ensuring that digital evidence can be appropriately used in investigations and legal proceedings.

Moving forward, a multi-faceted approach is crucial. It's not enough to simply address the immediate needs of victims; we must focus on building a system that prevents future tragedies. This necessitates a sustained and collaborative effort involving law enforcement, social service providers, mental health professionals, educators, and community organizations. The legacy of Gabby Petito should not be simply a story of loss, but a catalyst for transformative change.

This calls for concrete action on several fronts. Firstly, increased funding for victim support services is critical. Shelters, legal aid organizations, and counseling services are consistently under-resourced, leaving victims with limited options. Government funding, coupled with private donations and corporate social responsibility initiatives, should prioritize these critical services, ensuring their availability and accessibility across all communities, regardless of socioeconomic status or geographic location.

Secondly, comprehensive training for law enforcement personnel is essential. Officers need specialized training to effectively respond to domestic violence calls, understand the dynamics of abuse, and provide appropriate support to victims. This training should emphasize victim-centered approaches, de-escalation techniques, and the importance of recognizing the subtle signs of abuse. Furthermore, regular refresher courses and ongoing professional development are critical in ensuring that law enforcement remains equipped to handle the complexities of domestic violence cases.

Thirdly, we need to strengthen legal frameworks and improve access to justice. Legal aid services need increased funding and resources to ensure that victims have access to skilled legal representation. Laws related to domestic violence should be regularly reviewed and updated to reflect current realities, providing victims with greater protection and ensuring abusers are held accountable. The legal process itself needs to be streamlined to minimize delays and trauma for victims.

Fourthly, public awareness campaigns are crucial. Educational programs should be implemented at all levels, starting in schools and continuing into adulthood, to educate the public about the signs of domestic violence, the importance of bystander intervention, and the resources available to victims. These campaigns should utilize a variety of media to reach diverse populations, ensuring that crucial information is accessible to everyone.

Finally, and perhaps most importantly, we need to foster a culture of empathy and support. Breaking the cycle of violence requires a collective effort, one that starts with each individual making a conscious decision to challenge harmful norms, support victims, and hold abusers accountable. This involves speaking out against abuse, offering support to those who need it, and being an active participant in building a society that does not tolerate violence.

Gabby Petito's story, though tragically short, served as a stark reminder of the pervasive issue of domestic violence and the urgent need for change. The legacy of her life should be the creation of a nation where victims are empowered, protected, and supported. It's a challenge that demands not just attention, but active participation and sustained commitment from all of us. The call to action is clear: we must work together to build a future where such tragedies are unthinkable. The memory of Gabby serves as a constant, poignant reminder of the urgency and importance of this collective endeavor. Her death should not be in vain. It should be the turning point in our fight to eradicate domestic violence. The path ahead is challenging, but with collective action and unwavering determination, we can honor Gabby's memory by building a safer and more just world for all.

www.ingramcontent.com/pod-product-compliance
Lightning Source LLC
Chambersburg PA
CBHW032211040426
42449CB00005B/539